3.75

CELT, DRUID AND CULDEE

by

ISABEL HILL ELDER

(MERCH O LUNDAIN DERRI)

Foreword

by

THE RIGHT HON. LORD BRABAZON OF TARA,
P.C., G.B.E., M.C.

LONDON

THE COVENANT PUBLISHING CO., LTD.

6 Buckingham Gate, S.W.1.

1973

FOURTH EDITION REVISED

(Reprinted 1973)

Dedicated to

WINIFRED G. HEATH

Made and Printed in England by
STAPLES PRINTERS LIMITED
at their Rochester, Kent, establishment

CONTENTS

'The fact that claims to some noble lineage and also to other matters as just and well founded, always becomes known somehow or other, even if people try to conceal it, being like musk, which spreads its odour, although it is hidden.'

Abu Raihan Muhammad (Albiruni)
A.D. 973–1048.

'In Books lies the soul of the whole Past Time; the articulate audible voice of the Past, when the body and material substance of it has altogether vanished like a dream. . . . All that mankind has done, thought, gained or been; it is lying as in magic preservation in the pages of Books. They are the chosen possession of men.'

Thomas Carlyle

'As you grow ready for it, somewhere or other you will find what is needful for you in a book.'

George MacDonald

'Adventure on, for from the littlest clue
Has come whatever worth man ever knew.'

Masefield

FOREWORD

TO THE FOURTH EDITION

BY

THE RIGHT HON. LORD BRABAZON OF TARA, P.C., G.B.E., M.C.

I SINCERELY hope that many people will read this work by Mrs. Elder, as first of all it gives much information on early Britain which should be known, and secondly, just as important, it dispels so many erroneous beliefs such as that Britain was uncivilized compared with Rome, that the Druids were a mischievous sect, etc. In these days when the Church of England is flirting with Rome, it is of great interest to see the splendid fight waged in these Isles for independence of thought in Christianity and the continued disinclination to accept Rome as an arbiter of all things relative to the Faith.

Mrs. Elder, I notice, does not mention the agreeable legend that Jesus lived for many years at Glastonbury, nor does she accentuate the arrival of Joseph of Arimathea at Glastonbury where the first Christian church in the world was built. However, she does state what is little known and not nearly enough appreciated—the fact that Christianity as a

Church was born in this country before anywhere else, and that England was a professed Christian country one hundred years before Rome and, in fact, when Rome was persecuting Christians. She draws attention to the singular change, without any opposition, from Druidism to Christianity, which was understandable in that fundamentally they had no great difference in belief. An interesting point also is made as to the difference between the British Church and the Church of England.

The Church of England was originally, of course, Roman, founded by St. Augustine, and was turned Protestant by the powers that be in our country, but it has never been quite so independent in thought as the British Church that fought Rome over so many hundreds of years. The history of the British Church, described in the book as Culdich, is of outstanding interest and should be read by all, for it redounds to the credit of our islands.

I feel inclined to repeat the words said to St. Augustine by the Bishops of the British Church when they refused to admit that the Bishop of Rome was their superior:

'Be it known and declared that we all, individually and collectively, are in all humility prepared to defer to the Church of God, and to the Bishop of Rome, and to every sincere and godly Christian, so far as to love everyone according to his degree, in perfect charity, and to assist them all by word and in deed in becoming the children of God. But as for any other obedience, we know of none that he, whom you term the Pope, or Bishop of Bishops,

can demand. The deference we have mentioned we
are ready to pay to him as to every other Christian,
but in all other respects our obedience is due to the
jurisdiction of the Bishop of Caerleon, who is alone
under God our ruler to keep us right in the way of
salvation.'

Brave, splendid words that thrill us even now,
though spoken over a thousand years ago.

This is a thoughtful and absorbing book. I hope
indeed it will find a large public.

Brabazon of Tara

PREFACE

FROM a mass of material in which is intertwined legend, tradition, native history and the contributions of Greek and Roman writers to our ancient history, the present writer has endeavoured to create within the compass of this small volume a more favourable impression of the past history of the British Isles than that which is customarily received.

Fragmentary though the evidence may be, of an early British civilization and culture and a flourishing British Church, it should go far to stimulate sympathetic appreciation of those early ancestors whose untiring efforts in defence of country and religion resulted in a heritage for the British people of freedom and humanitarian principles.

There are many perversions of truth relative to the past which the British people have long since settled down to believe, with the result that the modern sceptic hastens to cover with the chilling mantle of disbelief any attempt to present a true account of early British affairs.

It may be said that intense patriotism has obscured the present writer's view to many imperfections in the character and practices of our ancestors; the creation of this impression, however, is almost impossible to avoid when the defence of ancient peoples is undertaken. So much that belittles and even defames the early Briton and exalts everything Roman has been written, and so little that presents the opposite view, that it seems unlikely the average reader will realize that our ancestors were neither barbarous nor idolatrous.

It has become a commonplace, in writing or conversing on the subject of the origin of religion and culture in these islands, to assume that it began about the beginning of the time of the Roman occupation, that the early inhabitants contributed nothing, that, in fact, the conditions which prevailed prior to the arrival of the Romans were such as would obtain among the lowest type of aboriginal savages. This unworthy mental attitude is the effect of a series of causes which began with the transmutation of Roman war propaganda into history.

The present writer undertook the study of early Christianity in our islands from a keen desire to ascertain how much we really do owe to the Romans in matters ecclesiastical (as well as civil) and in the hope that it might be possible to illuminate in some degree the obscurity which enshrouds this portion of our ancient story.

In the following chapters the reader will realize, it is hoped, that the Church came into being in a country with great features, national and political, and a great inheritance. To say that in Britain there were four ascending steps to Protestantism—William the Conqueror, Edward III, Wycliffe and the Reformation—is to state but part of the truth, and robs us of a thousand years of history of a struggle for Protestantism by which the four recognized ascending steps were made possible.

The rise and establishment of Christianity in Britain has been dealt with by so many writers that one hesitates to add yet another volume to a subject which has admittedly definite limitations in public interest. It may be, however, that in these pages will be found that new light has been thrown on the origin of the Culdees, with whom rests the introduction and, with their successors, the defence of Apostolic Christianity brought by these first Christians to this land shortly after the Ascension of our Lord.

In sending forth this, the fourth edition of *Celt, Druid and Culdee,* my very sincere thanks are due to the many readers who so kindly supported the earlier editions and for whose appreciation the writer will be ever grateful.

I. H. E.

CHAPTER I

THE EARLY BRITONS

IT has been said that the only excuse for writing a book is that one has something to say which has not been said before. That this claim cannot be made on behalf of this little volume will be very evident to the reader as he proceeds, since it is a compilation from a variety of sources, from which evidence has been brought together, to support the belief that the civilization of the early Britons was of a high standard, and that they did not deserve that contempt with which they have been treated by many historians, nor the odious names of 'savages' and 'barbarians' by the supercilious *literati* of Greece and Rome.

When evidence, admittedly fragmentary, of the real conditions in these islands, from the earliest times, has been brought to light throughout the centuries, it seems, almost invariably, to have been rejected in favour of Roman teaching.

In his *History of Scotland,* the Rev. J. A. Wylie, LL.D., says, 'We have been taught to picture the earliest conditions of our country as one of unbroken darkness. A calm consideration of the time and circumstances of its first peopling warrants a more cheerful view.'[1]

By examining the available evidence it may be possible to obtain this more cheerful view, and to show that in the darkest eras of our country the rites of public worship were publicly observed. It is ever true to say that, 'The history of a nation is the history of its religion, its attempts to seek after God.'

Wilford states that the old Indians were acquainted with the British Islands, which their books described as the sacred islands of the west, and called one of them Britashtan, or the seat or place of religious duty.[2]

The popular idea that the ancestors of the British were painted savages has no foundation in fact. It was a custom of the Picts and other branches of the Celtic and Gothic nations to make themselves look terrible in war, from whence came the Roman term 'savage'. The 'painting' was in reality tattooing, a practice still cherished in all its primitive crudities by the British sailor and soldier.

Far from these ancestral Britons having been mere painted savages, roaming wild in the woods as we are imaginatively told in most of the modern histories, they are now, on the contrary, as disclosed by newly-found historical facts given by Professor Waddell,[3] known to have been, from the very first grounding of their galley keels upon these shores, over a millennium and a half before the Christian era, a highly civilized and literate race, pioneers of civilization.

The universally held belief that the British are a mixed race has prevailed during many centuries; this belief, however, is now fading out of the scientific mind and giving place to the exact opposite. Britons, Celts, Gaels, Anglo-Saxons, Danes and Normans when warring with each other were kinsmen shedding kindred blood.

Professor Sayce, at a later date, in one of his lectures, observes that he misses no opportunity of uprooting the notion that the people who form the British nation are descended from various races, all the branches that flowed into Britain being branches of the selfsame stock. Not a single pure Saxon is to be found in any village, town or city of Germany. Our Saxon ancestors rested there for a time in their wandering to these islands.[4]

Dr. Latham says, 'Throughout the whole length and breadth of Germany there is not one village, hamlet or family which can show definite signs of descent from the Continental ancestors of the Angles of England.'[5]

It was against this race, now in possession of the whole of Southern Britain, that Caesar led his legions. The Belgae, the Attrebates, the Parisii and the Britanni were all British tribes, having kinsmen on the Continent, yet moving westward, who had fought against Caesar in the Gallic wars.[6]

It is noteworthy that during the occupation of Britain by the Romans the inhabitants led a life as separate as possible from their invaders and, according to Professor Huxley, when the Romans withdrew from Britain in A.D. 410 the population was as substantially Celtic as they found it. Huxley in 1870, in the earlier years of the Irish agitation, applied the results of his studies to the political situation in Ireland in the following words in one of his lectures, 'If what I have to say in a matter of science weighs with any man who has political power I ask him to believe that the arguments made about the difference between Anglo-

Saxons and Celts are a mere sham and delusion."[7]

The Welsh Triads and the 'Chronicum Regum Pictorum' as well as the 'Psalter of Cashel' give us the chief early information about the inhabitants of Scotland, and all agree as to the racial unity of the peoples, much, however, as they fought each other. This unity is recognized by Thierry,[8] Nicholas,[9] Palgrave[10] and Bruce Hannay.[11]

The Britons were renowned for their athletic form, for the great strength of their bodies, and for swiftness of foot. Clean-shaven, save for long moustaches, with fair skins and fair hair, they were a fine, manly race; of great height (Strabo tells us that British youths were six inches taller than the tallest man in Rome) and powerfully built. They excelled in running, swimming, wrestling, climbing and in all kinds of bodily exercise; were patient in pain, toil and suffering, accustomed to fatigue,[12] to bearing hunger, cold and all manner of hardships. Bravery, fidelity to their word, manly independence, love of their national free institutions, and hatred of every pollution and meanness were their notable characteristics.

Tacitus tells us the northern Britons were well trained and armed for war. In the battlefield they formed themselves into battalions; the soldiers were armed with huge swords and small shields called 'short targets', they had chariots and cavalry, and carried darts which they hurled in showers on the enemy. Magnificent as horsemen, with their chargers gaily caparisoned, they presented a splendid spectacle when prepared for battle. The cumulative evidence is of a people numerous, brave and energetic. Even Agricola could say that it would be no disgrace to him, were he to fall in battle, to do so among so brave a people.[13]

Farther south similar conditions prevailed; the Romans, led by Plautius and Flavius Vespasian, the future Emperor and his brother, assailed the British, and were met with the British 'stupidity' which never knows when it is beaten.

The British have been from all time a people apart, characterized by independence, justice and a love of religion. Boadicea, in her oration as queen by Dion Cassius, observes that though Britain had been for centuries open to the Continent, yet its language, philosophy and usages continued as great a mystery as ever to the Romans themselves.

The monuments of the ancient Britons have long since vanished (with the exception of Stonehenge and other places of Druidic worship), yet Nennius, the British historian who was Abbot of Bangor-on-Dee about A.D. 860, states that he drew the greater part of his information from writings and the monuments of the old British inhabitants.[14] Our early historians were undoubtedly acquainted with a book of annals written in the vernacular tongue which was substantially the same as the Saxon Chronicle.

Nennius disclaims any special ability for the task of historian set him by his superiors, but is filled with a keen desire to see justice done to the memory of his countrymen, saying, 'I bore about with me an inward wound, and I was indignant that the name of my own people, formerly famous and distinguished, should sink into oblivion and like smoke be dissipated.'[15] . . .

'It is better to drink a wholesome draught of truth

from a humble vessel than poison mixed with honey from a golden goblet.'[16]

What were once considered exaggerated statements on the part of Nennius, Geoffrey of Monmouth and other early historians, are now discovered to be trustworthy. In their day these writers were regarded as historians of repute. Many of the ancient British writers were professed genealogists, men appointed and patronized by the princes of the country, who were prohibited from following other professions.[17] It was left to a later age to throw doubt on their veracity. Since it is the nature of truth to establish itself it seems the reverse of scholarly to disregard the evidence of ancient reports as embodied in the Welsh Triads and the writings of early British historians.

Milton says, 'These old and inborn names of successive kings never to have been real persons, or done in their lives at least some part of what so long hath been remembered cannot be thought without too strict incredulity.[18]

A great deal of history, so-called, has come down to us from Latin sources, whose one object was, from the very first, to make us believe that we owe all to Rome, when, in fact, Rome owes a great deal to us; so much error has been taught in our schools concerning the ancient Britons that it is difficult for the average student to realize that the British, before the arrival of Julius Caesar, were, in all probability, among the most highly educated people on the earth at that time and, as regards scientific research, surpassed both the Greeks and the Romans—a fact testified to by both Greek and Roman writers themselves.[19]

In all the solid essentials of humanity our British ancestors compare to great advantage with the best eras of Greece and Rome.

Lumisden has shown in his treatise on the 'Antiquities of Rome' that many of the fine actions attributed by Roman historians to their own ancestors are mere copies from the early history of Greece.[20]

It is unfortunate for posterity that the histories from which modern historians have drawn their information were written by hostile strangers. That they have been accepted all along the centuries as true is a striking tribute to a people who, valiant in war and fierce in the defence of their rights, think no evil of their enemies. Truly has it been said that an essentially British characteristic is the swift forgetfulness of injury.

[1] *History of Scotland*, Vol. I, p. 31.
[2] *Asiatic Researches*, Vol. 3.
[3] *Origin of Britons, Scots and Anglo-Saxons*, p. 14.
[4] Hibbert Lectures (1887).
[5] *Ethnology of the British Islands*, p. 217.
[6] Gilbert Stone, *England*, p. 9.
[7] Anthrop. Rev. 1870, Vol. 8, p. 197, *Forefathers and Forerunners of the British People*.
[8] *Norman Conquest*, p. 20.
[9] *Pedigree of the English People*.
[10] Palgrave, *English Commonwealth*, Ch. I, p. 85.
[11] Hannay, *European and other Race Origins*, pp. 365, 470, 371.
[12] Pezron, *Antig, de la Nation et de la Langue Gaulaise*.
[13] Vita Agricolae, c. 28.
[14] *Historiae Brittonum* of Nennius, Harleian MS 3859 (British Museum).
[15] *Vide* Geoffrey of Monmouth, I, 1. See Cave *Hist. Lit.* II, 18.
[16] Nennius, *Hist. of the Britons*, trans. J. A. Giles, Prol. p. 2.
[17] Gir. Camb. *Cambriae Descript.*, Cap. XVIII. Anglica Hibernica, ed. Camden, p. 890.
[18] *History of England*, Vol. 8, p. 11.
[19] Strabo, I, IV, p. 197. Mela Pom., III, 2, 18. N.H., I, 30.
[20] *Antiq. of Rome*, pp. 6, 7, 8.

CHAPTER II

LAWS AND ROADS

THAT Britain had an indigenous system of law centuries before the Christian era is abundantly clear from the ancient histories of our islands.

The lawgiver, Molmutius, 450 B.C.,[1] based his laws on the code of Brutus, 1100 B.C. He was the son of Cloton, Duke of Cornwall (which was and continued to be a royal dukedom) and is referred to in ancient documents as Dyfn-val-meol-meod, and because of his wisdom has been called the 'Solomon' of Britain.

'Centuries before the Romans gained a footing in this country the inhabitants were a polished and intellectual people, with a system of jurisprudence of their own, superior even to the laws of Rome, and the Romans acknowledged this.'[2]

We have it from the great law authorities and from the legal writers, Fortescue and Coke, that the Brutus and Molmutine laws have always been regarded as the foundation and bulwark of British liberties, and are distinguished for their clearness, brevity, justice and humanity.[3]

'The original laws of this land were composed of such elements as Brutus first selected from the ancient Greek and Trojan institutions.'[4]

A Trojan law, mentioned by E. O. Gordon, decreed that the sceptre might pass to a queen as well as to a king; this law was embodied by King Molmutius in his code and remains an outstanding feature of the rulership of these islands.[5]

The liberty of the subject, so marked a feature of British government today, runs from those remote times like a gold thread through all the laws and institutions in this country.

King Alfred, it is recorded, employed his scribe, Asser, a learned Welsh monk from St. David's (whom he afterwards made Abbot of Amesbury and Bishop of Sherborne), to translate the Molmutine laws from the Celtic tongue into Latin, in order that he might incorporate them into his own Anglo-Saxon code.[6]

'The Manorial system had its beginning in Celtic Britain and was so deeply rooted in the soil that when the Romans came they were wise enough in their experience as colonists not to attempt the redistribution of the old shires and hundreds.'[7]

King Alfred's ideas of rulership maintained the earlier and sometimes unwritten laws of Britain in these words: 'A king's raw material and instruments of rule are a well-peopled land, and he must also have men of prayer, men of war and men of work.'

From the earliest Code of Laws known as the Molmutine, the following are appended as examples:

'There are three tests of civil liberty; equality of rights; equality of taxation; freedom to come and go.

'Three things are indispensable to a true union of nations; sameness of laws, rights and language.

'There are three things free to all Britons; the forest, the unworked mine, the right of hunting.

'There are three property birthrights of every Briton;

five British acres of land for a home, the right of suffrage in the enacting of the laws, the male at twenty-one, the female on her marriage.

'There are three things which every Briton may legally be compelled to attend; the worship of God, military service, the courts of law.

'There are three things free to every man, Briton or foreigner, the refusal of which no law will justify; water from spring, river or well; firing from a decayed tree, a block of stone not in use.

'There are three classes which are exempt from bearing arms; bards, judges, graduates in law or religion. These represent God and His peace, and no weapon must ever be found in their hands.

'There are three persons who have a right of public maintenance; the old, the babe, the foreigner who cannot speak the British tongue.'[8]

From time immemorial the laws and customs differed from those of other nations, and that the Romans effected no change in this respect is very plainly set forth by Henry de Bracton, a thirteenth-century English judge of great experience. 'He was thoroughly acquainted with the practice of the law. His "Note-Book" is our earliest and most treasured of law reports.'[9] Judge de Bracton states, 'Whereas in almost all countries they use laws and written right, England alone uses within her boundaries unwritten right and custom. In England, indeed, right is derived from what is unwritten which usage has approved. There are also in England several and divers customs according to the diversity of places, for the English have many things by custom which they have not by written law, as in divers countries, cities, boroughs and vills where it will always have to be enquired what is the custom of the place and in what manner they who allege the custom observe the custom.'[10]

Another point on which Britain differs from other countries is that she has ever maintained the Common Law which holds a person under trial innocent until proved guilty, whereas the Continental nations maintain the Civil Law which holds him guilty until proved innocent.

Molmutius, the first king in these islands to wear a crown of gold,[11] is said to have founded the city of Bristol, which he called Caer Odor, 'the City of the Chasm'. His son Belinus, who succeeded him, built a city where London now stands which he called Caer Troia, and also the first Thames Embankment. He constructed a sort of quay or port made of poles and planks, and erected a water-gate. That gate, the only gate admitting into London on the south side, became Belinus Gate or Belins Gate.[12]

Belinus lived to the age of eighty. When he died his body was burned (they did not call it cremation in those days) and his ashes were enclosed in a brazen urn, which was placed on top of the gate; henceforth it was Belin's Gate and it requires no undue stretch of imagination to see that Belin's Gate became Billingsgate.

Billingsgate enjoys the proud distinction of being the first Port of London, the only Port of London at that time, and thus the men of Billingsgate became the first Port of London Authority.

Cambria Formosa, daughter of Belinus, 373 B.C.,

greatly promoted the building of cities. She is said to have taught the women of Britain to sow flax and hemp and weave it into cloth. Her brother Gwrgan first built the city of Cambridge which he called Caer Gwrgan.[13]

In these early times Britain was a wealthy country, with fine cities, a well-organized national life, and an educated and civilized people.

The so-called Roman roads in Britain were constructed centuries before the Romans came to these islands. The Dover to Holyhead causeway, called Sarn Wydellin or Irish Road, later became corrupted into Watling Street; the Sarn Ikin, later Icknield Street, led from London northwards through the eastern district, and Sarn Achmaen from London to Menevia (St. David's).

These were causeways or raised roads (not mere trackways as sometimes erroneously stated), except where raised roads were impossible, and this accounts for the term 'Holloway' in some parts of the country.

Our roads were begun by Molmutius (c. 450 B.C.) and completed by his son Belinus. On their completion a law was enacted throwing open these roads to all nations and foreigners : 'There are three things free to a country and its borders; the roads, the rivers and the places of worship. These are under the protection of God and His peace.' In this law originated the term 'The King's Highway'.[14]

Writers who maintain that the British roads were simply unmade trackways seem unaware of the fact that the British were skilled charioteers; this fact, without other evidence, should go a long way to prove that the roads of ancient Britain were hard and well made. Charioteering is not brought to perfection on soft, boggy trackways, nor are chariots built without wheelwrights and other mechanics skilled in the working of iron and wood.

Only once before, in the war with Antiochus, 192 B.C., the Romans met with similar chariots, but never in any European country. The British chariot was built after the Eastern pattern, adorned with carved figures and armed with hooks and scythes. British chariots were prized possessions of the Romans.

Diodorus Siculus, 60 B.C., states, 'The Britons live in the same manner that the ancients did; they fight in chariots as the ancient heroes of Greece are said to have done in the Trojan wars. . . . They are plain and upright in their dealings, and far from the craft and subtlety of our countrymen. . . . The island is very populous. . . . The Celts never shut the doors of their houses; they invite strangers to their feasts, and when all is over ask who they are and what is their business.[15]

Britain, long before the Roman invasion, was famous for its breed of horses and the daring and accomplishment of its charioteers; and after the arrival of the Romans the large space given by their historians to the wars in Britain demonstrate the interest felt in them by the whole empire. Juvenal could suggest no news which would have[16] been hailed by the Roman people with more satisfaction than the fall of the British king Arviragus (Caractacus), a direct descendant of King Molmutius.

'Hath our great enemy,
Arviragus, the car-borne British king,
Dropped from his battle-throne?'

[1] *Ancient Laws of Cambria* (British Museum, 5805, A.A. 4).
Myv. Arch., Vol. II, Brut Tysillo.

[2] Yeatman, *Early English History*, p. 9.

[3] De Laudibus Legum Angliae. Coke Preface, third volume
of Pleadings. Fortescue *Brit. Laws,* published with notes by
Selden, Ch. 17, pp. 38, 39.

[4] Ibid.

[5] *Prehistoric London*, p. 115.

[6] Summarized by Edmund Spenser, *Faerie Queen*, Bk. II,
Stanza XXXIX (ed. Morris).

[7] *A Manor through four Centuries*, by A. R. Cook.

[8] *Triads of Dynvall Moëlmud*, ap. Walter p. 315. Myv Arch.,
Vol. III. *Ancient Laws of Cambria*, ap. Palgrave and Lappenberg.

[9] Gilbert Stone, *England from Earliest Times*, p. 385.

[10] *Legibus et Consuet*, pp.4, 5.

[11] Holinshed, *Chronicles*, Ch. XXII, p. 117. Geoffrey of
Monmouth, Bk. II, Chap. XVII.

[12] E. O. Gordon, *Prehistoric London*, p. 146.

[13] Lewis, *Hist. of Britain*, p. 52. See Baker's MSS. in the
University Library, Cambridge, XXIV, 249.

[14] *Ancient Laws of Cambriae* (British Museum, A.A.4).
Stukely, *Abury*, p. 42.

[15] Dio. Sic., Bk. V, Chap. X. Senchus Mor., IV, 237.

[16] Juvenal lived through the reigns of Caligula, Claudius,
Nero, Vespasian, Domitian and Trojan, in whose reign he died
at the age of eighty.

CHAPTER III

COMMERCE AND DRESS

TACITUS and Strabo describe Londinium as famous
for the vast number of merchants who resorted to it
for its widely extended commerce, for the abundance
of every species of commodity which it could supply,
and they make note of British merchants bringing to
the Seine and the Rhine shiploads of corn and cattle,
iron and hides, and taking back iron, ivory and brass
ornaments.[1]

That Londinium was considered by the Romans as
the metropolis of Britain is further established by the
fact that it was the residence of the Vicar of Britain.[2]
The abode of such an office clearly marks London as
having been a seat of justice, of government and of
the administration of the finances which consequently
contributed to its extent, its magnificence and its
wealth.[3] Britain was, in fact, from at least 900 B.C. to
the Roman invasion, the manufacturing centre of the
world.

The Abbé de Fontenu proved that the Phoenicians,
the name by which the tribe of Asher was known after
Conquest of the Phoenician territory, had an established trade with Britain before the Trojan war, 1190
B.C.[4] Admiral Himilco of Carthage, who visited Britain
about the sixth century B.C. to explore 'the outer parts
of Europe', records that the Britons were a 'powerful

race, proud-spirited, effectively skilful in art, and constantly busy with the cares of trade'.[5]

Nor was Ireland less forward than Britain, for from the ancient Greek records it would appear that trade routes both by sea and land existed in these very early times, the latter route being across Europe through the territories of the Scythians. A most curious belief of the Greeks was that the inspiration which led to the institution of the Olympic Games was derived from the observance of ancient Irish festivities.[6]

The British farmer had a market for his produce beyond the shores of Britain. We learn from Zosimus that in the reign of Julian, A.D. 363, eight hundred pinnaces were built in order to supply Germany with corn from Britain.[7]

When the Romans invaded Britain in A.D. 43 they found the inhabitants in possession of a gold coinage, and of beautifully wrought shields of bronze[8] and enamelled ornaments.[9] Fine specimens of richly enamelled horses' trappings may be seen in the British Museum, and the bronze shield found in the Thames, near Battersea, adorned with enamelled designs, Rice Holmes describes as 'the noblest creation of late Celtic art'.[10]

The beautiful brooches discovered in different parts of these islands clearly demonstrated that the Britons were skilful and artistic metal workers, and in the centuries of Roman domination the Celtic patterns did not die out. A peculiarly Celtic type is the 'dragon' brooch 'representing a conventionalized writhing dragon, often magnificently inlaid with enamel, and recalling in its vigorous design and curvilinear motives all the essential qualities of late Celtic art'. Thus the native tradition of metal work continued under Roman rule to flourish and to produce types which were not merely Roman but recognizably Celtic.[11] In a further description of these brooches Mr. Collingwood says, 'In the true Celtic spirit the ornament on the trumpet head is often made with eyes and nostrils to resemble the head of an animal, but however the brooch is finished in detail it is always a masterpiece of both design and manufacture.'[12]

Enamelling was an art unknown to the Greeks until they were taught it by the Celts.[13]

Dr. Arthur Evans tells us that the Romans carried off some of the Britons to Rome to teach them the art of enamelling as well as that of glass-making.

Stukeley, giving an account of a glass urn discovered in the Isle of Ely in the year 1757, observes that the Britons were famous for glass manufacture.[14]

The early Britons were workers in pottery, turnery, smelting and glasswork.[15] In the excavations at Glastonbury well-made instruments of agriculture were found such as tools, files, safety-pins and also the remains of wells and bridges.

The British tin mines were, from the earliest times, world renowned. Diodorus Siculus states, 'These people obtain the tin by skilfully working the soil which produces it.'[16]

Herodotus speaks of the British Isles under the general term Cassiterides or the Tin Islands.[17] Bede mentions copper, iron, lead and silver. 'Gold, too, was mined on a small scale in Wales, and on a large scale in Ireland where was situated in early times the centre of the goldmining industry.' Bede mentions also, as semi-precious, the jet for which Whitby is famous even now.[18]

The lead mines of Britain were worked long before the Roman occupation, and it is believed that during the partial domination by Rome the mining continued to be carried out by Celtic workmen.[19]

Dr. John Phillips, the geologist, stated in 1855 that without due consideration being given to the lead-mining industry, our ideas 'of the ancient British people would be altogether conjectural, derogatory and erroneous'.[20] Derbyshire was the chief centre of lead-mining, and is so mentioned in Domesday Book.

Eumenius, A.D. 266, private secretary to Constantius Chlorus, states, 'Britain is full of skilled craftsmen.'[21]

The coins of ancient Britain are worthy of more than passing notice. Numismatists tell us that our ancient British types cannot amount to many less than four hundred in number, of which possibly two hundred may have inscriptions;[22] this variety is to be accounted for by the fact that each tribe had its own stamped currency in gold, silver and bronze.

Canon Lysons states, 'It is to be remembered that the earliest British coins are not imitations of the Roman coinage, they much resemble the coinage of Philip of Macedon, Alexander the Great, and the Greek and Eastern mintage.'[23]

Dr. Borlase in his *Antiquites of Cornwall* asserts that the wheel under the horse seen on Cornish coins intimated the making of a highway for carts, and that the wheel is common on the coins of Cunobelinus,

14 B.C., on those of Cassebelinus, 51 B.C., and also on the Cornish coins which from their character appear to be older than the rest.

Sir John Evans devotes sixty-four pages of his standard work *Ancient British Coins* to the coins of Cunobelinus and the history of his reign.

That Cunobelinus, the Cymbeline of Shakespeare, was a man of education and refinement is well borne out by his coins, universally considered to be a true index and reflection of the mind. Numismatists tell us that the Cunobelinus types are by no means a Roman type and could hardly have been struck except by express command.[24]

The coins of Arviragus, son of Cunobelinus, are, where they are included, the gems of every collection.

The horse, sometimes thought to have been introduced as a national emblem by the Saxons, is one of the most common types upon the coins of the ancient Britons.

M. de la Saussaye, in describing the gold coin assigned to the British Druid Abaris, who visited Greece, mentioned by Hecataeus, states, 'I have been induced to modify my assertion on more than one point and I particularly recognize religious ideas peculiar to the Celts expressed on their monetary uninscribed types.'[25]

The palm trees on the coins of the Southern Belgae, who settled in Kent, Sussex, Hants, Wilts, Dorset and Devon proclaim the Eastern origin of these people.

From the modern pictorial representation of our ancestors we are expected to believe that their dress consisted of an animal skin fastened round the waist, and that they wandered, thus scantily clad, about their island home, living on nuts and berries.

Boadicea, Queen of the Iceni (the inhabitants of Norfolk and Suffolk), was described by Dion Cassius as a woman of commanding appearance. 'Her stature exceeded the ordinary height of women; her aspect was calm and collected, but her voice had become deep and pitiless. Her hair falling in long golden tresses as low as her hips was collected round her forehead by a golden coronet; she wore a "tartan" dress fitting closely to the bosom, but below the waist expanding in loose folds, as a gown; over it was a chlamys or military cloak. In her hand she bore a spear.'[26]

In these descriptions of native dress it is interesting to note the early use of the tartan. A British hooded cloak was evidently regarded by the Romans as a superior garment, for in Diocletian's Edict of Prices issued in A.D. 301, the price of the British cloak was the highest on the list, with the exception of the Gallic. If the price was high on account of the quality of the wool, the statement of the epigrammatist, Martial, A.D. 60, is given as substantiating that among other attractions, Britain was 'for wool past compare'.[27]

Ireland kept pace with Britain in the farming for wool, both for export and domestic use; 'the Irish cottiers were always warmly clad in their own home-spuns.'[28]

The Briton in battledress was an impressive figure, being clad precisely as were the men of Gaul; clean-shaven, save for long moustaches, with fair skins and fair hair, gorgeously clad in breeches, bright-coloured tunics and woollen cloaks dyed crimson and often of a chequered pattern with torques, armlets and bracelets of gold, shields of enamelled bronze, and swords of fine workmanship, they presented a splendid spectacle when prepared for battle.

The Britons appear to have been also importers of cloth. According to one authority, Phoenician cloths of Beyrout were largely worn by the inhabitants of ancient Britain. At Beyrout our Patron Saint George held for a time an important post under the Roman Government.[29]

A torque or gold collar was worn by the wealthier inhabitants, and worn also as a distinguishing sign of eminence.[30] Specimens of these torques have been discovered from time to time, and may be seen in various museums, notably Dublin National Museum, and in private collections. A very good example acquired by the late Duke of Westminster and deposited at Eaton Hall was found at Bryn Sion Caerwys Mill; it is thirty-two inches long and weighs twenty-four ounces.

[1] Strabo, *Geogr.* III, 175; IV, 199.
[2] A Roman office.
[3] Amm. Marcell, Lib. 15, Chaps. 8, 9.
[4] *Mem. de Littérature*, tome VII, p. 126.
[5] Fragment preserved by Festus Avienus, *Ora Maritama*, V, 98–100.
[6] C. F. Parker, *On the Trail of Irish Identity. National Message*, March 8, 1939.
[7] Zosimus, Lib. III, p. 43 (Ed. Bas.).
[8] Philostratus. A Greek sophist (third century) who resided at Court of Julia Domna, describes the British process.
[9] Gilbert Stone, *England from Earliest Times*, p. 10.
[10] *Anc. Brit.*, p. 244.
[11] R. C. Collingwood, *Roman Britain*, p. 76.
[12] *Archaeology of Roman Britain*, p. 253.
[13] J. Romilly Allen, *Celtic Art*, p. 136.
[14] Minutes of Antiq. Soc., March 1762.

15 *Gallic Antiq.*, p. 64 (J. Smith).
16 Bk. V, Chap. X.
17 *Thalia*, Section C, XV (Bel. ed.).
18 Gilbert Stone, *England from Earliest Times*, p. 15.
19 Gordon Home, *Roman York*, p. 27.
20 Yorks Philos. Soc., Vol. I, p 92.
21 *Panegyric Constanteus*, C, III.
22 J. Evans, *Coins of the Anc. Brit.*, O, 171.
23 *Our British Ancestors*, p. 41.
24 *Coins of Cunobelinus and of the Ancient Britons*, p 26.
25 *La Revue Numismatique*, for 1842, p. 165.
26 Dion Cassius (Xiphilinus Excerpta), p. 176. See Strabo, Bk. IV, Chap. IV, 3.
27 Martial, Lib. I, ep. 2; and Lib. III, ep. 20.
28 Stephen Gwynn, *History of Ireland*, p. 330.
29 Rev. Canon Parfitt, M.A., *St. George of Merry England*, 1917.
30 Gibson's *Camden*, p. 653. Hoare, *Ancient Wilts*, Vol. I, p. 202.

CHAPTER IV

THE ROMAN INVASION

AT the time of the Roman invasion evidence of prosperity and culture existed in Britain to arouse the envy of the Romans, and it is a matter of history that the inhabitants led a life as separate as possible from them.

It was only after ten years' incessant warfare that the Romans in A.D. 43 succeeded in effecting a footing in Britain. This is not reconcilable with the view that the Romans were invading the territory of untrained, undisciplined savages. The resistance of Britain was, in reality, against the whole of the north of Europe, and was highly creditable to the brave defenders of their country. In the immortal words of Shakespeare in his *Cymbeline,* 'Caesar made not here his boast of came and saw and overcame.'[1]

To estimate aright the military abilities of the British general, Caswallon, and the resources of the people at the period of the first collision of our island with the Continent, it should be borne in mind that they were engaged against, perhaps, the ablest general of antiquity. The double repulsion of the Julian expedition, 55 and 54 B.C., remains unparalleled in British history.

In Britain there was one supreme Crown and three Coronets or Princes' Crowns; there were numerous other 'kings' who never wore crowns.

The sovereign who reigned in Britain at the time of the Claudian invasion was Cunobelinus, or King Belinus, the Cymbeline of Shakespeare. Cuno, Cun and Can have their equivalents in the Saxon Cynig; in modern German, Konig, and in English, King.

Cunobelinus and his ancestors had much intercourse with the Romans; he is said to have spent the greater part of his boyhood at the Court of Rome.[2]

The Roman invasion of his reign was met by Cunobelinus and his sons with a stubbornness of defence and bravery which earned for them the admiration of the enemy and aroused the wonder of all Europe.

Cunobelinus, after a reign of thirty years, abdicated in favour of his third son, Caradoc (Caractacus), who now became Arviragus or high king and by this title is most frequently referred to in the British Chronicles.

Tacitus reluctantly tells us that, 'In Britain after the capture of Caractacus (Arviragus) the Romans were frequently defeated and put to rout by the single state of the Silures alone.'[3] The Silures, the inhabitants of south-west Britain, were noted for their military prowess and culture.

It is evident from the partial story furnished by the invaders themselves that the resistance offered by the Britons to their invaders was a surprise for which they were ill-prepared, for this resistance came not from hordes of savages but from a nation whose leaders were well versed in military tactics. The Britons were determined to defend their ancient laws and institutions at all costs. They evinced profound homage for the memory of their forefathers, and from their inborn love of liberty sprang the undaunted energy with which they met the mercenary and implacable plunderers of the world. By no people was every inch of the country contested with more bravery and surrendered more stubbornly than by these Britons; on terms, indeed, which rendered every victory for the Romans little better than defeat.[4] It is absurd to suppose that such a nation could be barbarous.

If popular amusements are to be taken as the test the Romans were themselves the most barbarous of the nations of Europe. When the brutal sports of the gladiators were proposed to be introduced at Athens even the cynics cried out, 'We must first pull down the statue to mercy which our forefathers erected fifteen hundred years ago.'

A similar gulf separated the British from the Roman temper, and the comparison of the latter people with regard to the former should be received with the caution which we would exercise today in receiving the accounts of hostile strangers.

All the evidence supplied by Caesar refutes the notion of material barbarism. Agriculture was universal, corn everywhere abundant, pasturage a distinct branch of national wealth, and the population so numerous as to excite his astonishment—*hominum, multitudo infinito*—the surest and most satisfactory proof of a sound social state and ample means of sustenance.[5]

Having effected a landing (and the testimony of their own historians is that never was country more dearly purchased nor held with greater difficulty) the Romans proceeded with their policy of destruction for which they had become notorious on the continent of Europe.

One notable instance has come down to us of the Roman spirit of cruel indifference to human feelings and sufferings. The immensely wealthy Prasutagus, King of the Iceni, apprehensive, in the event of his death, of the Roman brutality likely to be experienced by his queen, Boadicea, and his two daughters, left one half of his fortune to the Emperor Nero, endeavouring thus to secure for them a measure of protection. When, however, his death took place in A.D. 60, the Roman *praefect*, Caius Decius, seized the royal hoard on the pretext that it came under the denomination of public property. Resistance being made, the legionaries stormed the palace and carried the treasures off to the Castra.[6] The story of the barbarous treatment meted out to its inmates need not be repeated here, nor of Boadicea, stung to frenzy by these atrocities, bravely taking to the field in defence of her family and her people, the Roman *praefect* having, in direct violation of the Claudian treaty, also confiscated the estates of the Icenic nobility.

Seneca, the usurious, millionaire philosopher, advanced to the Iceni, on the security of their public buildings, a sum of money—about two million pounds sterling in modern currency, at ruinous rates;[7] this loan, suddenly and violently called in, was the indirect cause of the Boadicean war. It was a disgrace for a Roman to lend to a Roman for interest; they were permitted, however, to lend to a foreigner.

The territories of the Iceni were rich in lead-mines, some of which were known to have been worked in times of even greater antiquity; the Romans seized these mines soon after their arrival in Britain, thus cutting off an important source of the wealth of the Icenic people and obliging them to borrow money from Seneca for the maintenance of their state.[8]

Boadicea, before leading her people and the tribe of the Trinobantes who joined them, to war, to redress her wrongs, ascended the 'generals'' tribunal and addressed her army of 120,000 in these words : 'I rule not like Nitocris, over beasts of burden, as are the effeminate nations of the East, nor, like Semiramis, over tradesmen and traffickers, nor like the man-woman, Nero, over slaves and eunuchs—such is the precious knowledge such foreigners introduce amongst us—but I rule over Britons, little versed, indeed, in craft and diplomacy, but born and trained to the game of war; men who in the cause of liberty stake down their lives, the lives of their wives and children, their lands and property—Queen of such a race, I implore your aid for freedom, for victory over enemies infamous for the wantonness of the wrongs they inflict, for their perversion of justice, for their insatiable greed; a people that revel in unmanly pleasures, whose affections are more to be dreaded and abhorred than their enmity. Never let a foreigner bear rule over me or over my countrymen; never let slavery reign in this island.'[9]

Boadicea's many successful engagements with the Roman armies are recorded in our histories, and when her death took place in Flintshire, after her eventual defeat, the Romans were impressed with the extraordinary magnificence of her obsequies. According to

Tacitus[10] Boadicea died by poison; in the course of nature according to the Greek historian, Dion Cassius.

Boadicea's kinsman, Caradoc, on meeting the invading Romans, displayed a like spirit of bravery and courage; perhaps indeed no warrior of ancient times succeeded in winning so much admiration from the enemy as this king of the south-western Britons, better known by his Latinized name of Caractacus.

The Welsh or Cymry, as the eldest tribe, held three priorities. Priority as the first colonizers of Britain; priority of government and priority in matters of learning and culture.[11] From this premier tribe was to be elected the Pendragon, or military dictator with absolute power for the time being in the case of national danger or foreign invasion. Caractacus, third son of Cunobelinus, had now succeeded his father as Pendragon under the title Arviragus, or 'high king'.

This Pendragon was proudly referred to by his fellow countrymen as 'The Praiseworthy Opposer'. Arviragus had yet another name, Gueirydd (Justiciary), from his office of administrator of justice, and by this name is mentioned in the Welsh Chronicles.

These three titles by which this ancient king of renown was known have been a source of confusion in the minds of historical students and others, which would not exist if the custom of the ancient Britons, that of using titular designations, were better known. The case under consideration is a good example of this custom; in elucidation the following may be noted : in seven genealogical charts setting forth his pedigree, Arviragus is shown to be the son of Cunobelinus and grandsire of Lucius (in whose reign

Christianity was established as the national religion); in the pedigree according to the classics, i.e. Julius Caesar, Tacitus, Suetonius, Dion Cassius and Orosius, Caractacus is shown to be the son of Cunobelinus; in Rome Caractacus was known also by his title, Arviragus, and is so referred to by the poet Juvenal. In the pedigree according to Tysilio and in the Welsh Chronicles, Caractacus appears under his title Gueirdd (Justiciary), son of Cunobelinus and grandsire of Lucius. Further, in the Triads, and some of the Welsh genealogies, Caractacus appears as the son of Bran and grandsire of Lucius. Bran, a contraction of Brenhan, i.e. 'King', is mentioned in the Triads as 'Bran the Blessed' (the Blessed King). This was the designation of Cunobelinus following his acceptance of Christianity and his resignation of the crown in favour of his third son, Caractacus. Bran the Blessed became Archdruid of Siluria in order to devote the remainder of his life to Christianity into which Druidism was beginning to merge.

Caradoc (Caractacus) was no rude savage fighting out of mere animal instinct or in ignorance of the might of his adversary. Familiar with the Latin language, this king was a true representative of the higher classes of the Britons, 'among whom a general taste for literature, a keen susceptibility to all intellectual gratifications, a minute acquaintance with all the principles and practice of their own national jurisprudence, and a careful training in the schools of the rhetoricians, was very generally diffused. Hence the rejoicing at Rome when this military leader was betrayed and subsequently conducted through the capital, amidst the excitement of three million inhabitants who thronged the line of procession to obtain a view of the formidable captive'. The Senate was convened; the famous trial of Caradoc followed, in which before the tribunal of the Emperor he delivered himself thus: 'Had my government in Britain been directed solely with a view to the preservation of my hereditary domains, or the agrandisement of my own family, I might, long since, have entered this city an ally, not a prisoner; nor would you have disdained for a friend, a prince, descended from illustrious ancestors, and the dictator of many nations. My present condition, stripped of its former majesty, is as adverse to myself as it is a cause of triumph to you. What then? I was lord of men, arms, horses, wealth: What wonder if at your dictation I refuse to resign them! Does it follow that because the Romans aspire to universal dominion every nation is to accept the vassalage they would impose? I am now in your power, betrayed, not conquered. Had I, like others, yielded without resistance, where would have been the name of Caradoc [Caractacus]? Where your glory? Oblivion would have buried both in the same tomb. Bid me live. I shall survive for ever in history, one example at least of Roman clemency.'

The preservation of Caradoc forms a solitary exception in the long catalogue of victims to the merciless policy of Imperial Rome. His life was spared on condition that he never again bore arms against Rome. After a residence of seven years in free custody in Rome he was permitted to return to Britain.

The British prince, Caradoc, in maintaining his

descent from illustrious ancestors, could bring from the clan records evidence of his pedigree; in those remote times genealogies were guarded with extreme care and recorded with exactitude by the herald-bard of each clan.[12]

On the public reception of a child, at the age of fifteen, into the clan, his genealogy was proclaimed and challengers of it commanded to come forward.

Pedigree and inheritance were so identified in the ancient British code that an heir even in the ninth descent could redeem at a valuation by jury any portion of an estate with which his forefathers had been compelled to part.[13]

All the family of Caradoc were attached to literary pursuits; copies of the best Greek and Roman authors were circulated in Siluria and deposited in the chief centres of Druidic learning.[14]

Caradoc's daughter, Claudia, who with other members of her family remained in Rome as hostages during her father's captivity there, wrote several volumes of hymns and odes.[15] Her praises were sung by the poet Martial:

'Our Claudia named Rufina, sprung we know
From blue-eyed Britons; yet behold, she vies
In grace with all that Greece or Rome can show.
As bred and born beneath their glowing skies.'

In a later epigram Martial writes:

'For mountains, bridges, rivers, churches and fair
women, Britain is past compare.'[16]

Caradoc's sister, 'Pomponia Grecina', received her

cognomen through her acquaintance with Greek literature, while her aunt, Blonwen, daughter of Cunobelinus, is believed to be the Imogen of Shakespeare in his *Cymbeline*. The great poet immortalized this ancient British king in the lines :

> 'The lofty cedar, royal Cymbeline personates thee.'[17]

The state of the country of the northern Britons is indicated by the number of large cities beyond the Forth which Agricola explored with his fleet. This could not mean cities which he had erected, he having been only six years in the country, nor could cities have arisen in that period, *'amplas civitates'*, as we learn from his biographer, Tacitus.

In a general account of Britain, Ptolemy, in A.D. 110, enumerates fifty-six cities; later, Marcianus enumerated fifty-nine.

It was not until the reign of Hadrian, A.D. 120, that Britain was incorporated by treaty, not conquest, with the Roman dominions;[18] the Britons retained their kings, land, laws and rights, and accepted a Roman nucleus of the army for the defence of the realm. These local kings and princes of Britain were obliged to become lieutenants of the Roman Emperor, just as the heads of our countries are now styled lieutenants of the Sovereign. They were bound to permit the construction of a Roman *castra* garrisoned by Roman legionaries, with their usual staff of engineers, in their chief city. On the ruins of British buildings and monuments rose the Roman *castras* and villas, the remains of which are treasured by many in this country who appear to be quite unaware of the earlier civilization.

The buildings erected by the Romans were foreign to British ideas and never became an integral part of British life.

When Alaric and his Goths were engaged in the sack of Rome, the Britons remembered their ancient independence and their brave ancestors; and having armed themselves, they threw off the Roman yoke, deposed the imperial magistrates and proclaimed their insular independence. The Emperor Honorius sent letters addressed to the *civitates* of Britain, clearing them from the responsibility of being any part of the Roman world.[19]

The Romans came to a country which was in all its essentials prosperous and free. They left it in many places devastated. Roman policy is tersely summed up in the words of the Pictish sovereign Galgacus, 'To robbery, slaughter, plunder, the Romans give the lying name of Empire; they make a solitude and call it peace.'[20]

The Roman imperial system had its strong points, but it had many weak ones—the two main weak points were war and slavery. With the Romans war became the instrument of progress, but it was a system fatal to real progress and to the domestic virtues. To plough the soil and wait for the harvest seemed to them a spiritless method of acquiring that which might more easily be obtained by conquest. Eloquence and the affairs of government as well as the exciting and barbarous sports of the arena, were esteemed and valued by Rome more than religion; hence her basilicas and her amphitheatres were far more spacious and magnificent than her temples.

The temper of the Britons may be judged by the evidence of the important part a non-idolatrous religion exercised in their daily lives; it has been said that the history of Britain is written in her churches. This truism is applicable from the most remote times, and from the nature of ancient worship it is possible to discover the source of the uprightness, the independence and the tolerance which characterized the early Britons.

These characteristics were noted by the Romans without their effecting the least check on unprincipled avarice and ambition. Salvian, A.D. 430, does not hesitate to say that the barbarians (so-called) led better lives than the Romans, even of those who were orthodox. 'Their modesty', he says, 'purifies the earth all stained by Roman debauchery.'[21] Amid the calamities and sufferings of the first invasion of Rome by our Gothic ancestors in A.D. 402, St. Augustine of Hippo remarked upon the marvellous forbearance of the soldiers of Alaric before the tombs of the Christian martyrs; he even went so far as to speak of the mercy and humility of these terrible victors.

To British genius alone we owe the foundation of our modern civilization, including roads, laws, learning and a culture of world-wide fame for more than two thousand years. From a more accurate knowledge of British history we shall gain some notion of that primeval liberty and self-government, common at first to the early Britons and preserved today by the British people.

That the Britons adopted anything they thought

good from the Romans is perfectly true; they did not, however, abandon any of their old essential laws and customs and still less their religion. But it is as untrue to say that the Britons had no previous civilization of their own as it is to pretend that Roman laws and customs permanently established themselves in Britain and remained after the legions were withdrawn. There is sufficient evidence to prove that the ancestors of the British, centuries before the Romans gained a footing in these islands, were a polished and intellectual people, skilled in arms as well as in learning, with a system of jurisprudence of their own superior even to the laws of Rome.[22]

To these early Britons we owe what we prize most —freedom, knowledge and a higher sense of right and wrong. This goodly heritage comes to us neither from a Roman conquest nor through Roman influence.

Montalembert declares: 'It is in England that the nobility of man's nature has developed all its splendour and attained its highest level. It is there that the generous passion of independence, united with the genius of association and the constant practice of self-government, have produced those miracles of fierce energy, of dauntless courage and obstinate heroism which have triumphed over seas and climate, time and distance, nature and tyranny, exciting the perpetual envy of all nations, and among the English themselves a proud enthusiasm.

It is not, however, for the British to pride themselves as a superior race, but rather that they are a ministering people, and that through them should flow the blessings of peace and goodwill to all the nations

of the world; loving freedom for itself, and loving
nothing without freedom. . . . Upon herself alone
weighs the formidable responsibility of her history.'[23]

'Love thou thy land with love far brought
From out the storied Past, and used
Within the Present, but transfused
Thro' future time by power and thought—
True love turned round on fix'd poles
Love, that endures not sordid ends
For English natures, freemen, friends,
Thy brothers, and immortal souls.'

Tennyson

[1] Act. V, Sc. 1.
[2] Ibid.
[3] *Annals*, XII, 38, 39.
[4] Beale Post, *Britannic Researches*, p. 74.
[5] Rev. R. W. Morgan, *St. Paul in Britain*, p. 79.
[6] Tacitus, *Annals*, XIV, 31.
[7] Dion Cassius (Xiphilinus Excepta).
[8] Beale Poste, *Britannic Researches*, p. 411.
[9] Dion Cassius (Xiphilinus Excepta).
[10] *Annals*, XIV, 37.
[11] Triads of the Cymry.
[12] *Anglica Hibernia*, ed. Camden, p. 890.
[13] Richard of Cirencester, Bk. I, Chap. III, note.
[14] Rev. R. W. Morgan, *St. Paul in Britain*, p. 104.
[15] Collier's *Eccl. History*, Bk. I.
[16] Martial, IV, 13; XI, 54.
[17] *Cymbeline*, Act 5, Sc. 1.
[18] Spartian's *Vita Hadrian*, Chap. I.
[19] Zosimus VI, pp. 376, 381. Also du Bos, Gibbon, Procopius, Gildas and Bede.
[20] Tacitus, *Vita Agricola*, XXX.
[21] *On the government of God*, Salvian.
[22] John Pym Teatman, *Early English History*, p. 9.
[23] *Monks of the West*, Vol. II, pp. 366, 367.

CHAPTER V

DRUIDISM

THE popular belief that Druidism was the religion of ancient Britain and nothing more is entirely erroneous. Druidism was, in fact, the centre and source from which radiated the whole system of organized civil and ecclesiastical knowledge and practice of the country.[1]

The Order constituted its church and parliament; its courts of law, its colleges of physicians and surgeons, its magistracy and clergy. The members of the Order were its statesmen, legislators, priests, physicians, lawyers, teachers and poets.

The truth about the Druids, to be found amongst fragments of literature and in folk-memory, is that they were men of culture, well-educated, equitable and impartial in the administration of justice. These ancient leaders of thought and instruction in our islands had lofty beliefs as to the character of the one God, Creator and Preserver, and of man's high origin and destiny. There is reason to believe that this doctrine included the need for atonement for sin and the resurrection of the body.

To reverence the Deity, abstain from evil and behave valiantly were, according to Laertius, the three grand articles enjoined by the Druids.[2]

In Druidism the British nation had a high standard of religion, justice and patriotism presented to it, and a code of moral teaching that has never ceased to influence national character.

It has been frequently stated that the name Druid is derived from Drus, an oak; the oak was held by the Druids to symbolize the Almighty Father, self-existent and eternal. The idea arose from the apparent similarity of the two words, Drus and Druid, and was merely incidental. A much more likely derivation is from Druthin, a servant of Truth.[3]

The motto of the Druidic Order, 'The Truth Against the World', was the principle on which Druidism was based and by which it offered itself to be judged.

'It may be asked,' says the Venerable Archdeacon Williams, 'how has it come to pass, if great events marked the epoch between the departure of the Romans and the death of Bede, that the whole history is so obscure, and that no literary documents remain to prove the wisdom of the teachers and the docility of the people? The answer is very plain. Such documents do exist; they have been published for more than half a century, but have hitherto wanted an adequate interpreter.'[4]

The published compositions of the Druids and Bards form but a very small portion of the extant remains of their works. The Myvyrian MSS. alone, now in the British Museum, amount to 47 volumes of poetry, containing about 4,700 pieces of poetry, in 1,600 pages, besides about 2,000 epigrammatic stanzas. Also in the same collection are 53 volumes of prose, in about 15,300 pages, containing many curious documents on various subjects, being 17th or 18th century compilations embodying early writings. Besides there are a vast number of collections of Welsh MSS. in London and in private libraries in the Principality.[5]

In A.D. 383 Druidism, while accepting Christianity, submitted to the judgment and verdict of country and nation the ancient privileges and usages; the ancient learning, sciences and memorials were confirmed, lest they should fail, become lost and forgotten—this was done without contradiction or opposition.'[6]

The educational system adopted by the Druids is traced to about 1800 B.C. when Hu Gadarn Hysicion (Isaacson),[7] or Hu the Mighty, led the first colony of Cymri into Britain from Defrobane, where Constantinople now stands.[8] In the justly celebrated Welsh Triads, Hu Gadarn is said to have mnemonically systematized the wisdom of the ancients of these people whom he led west from the Summerland. He was regarded as the personification of intellectual culture and is commemorated in Welsh archaeology for having made poetry the vehicle of memory, and to have been the inventor of the Triads. To him is attributed the founding of Stonehenge, and the introduction of several arts including glass-making and writing in Ogham characters. On Hu Gadarn's standard was depicted the Ox; in this possibly may be discovered the origin of the sobriquet, 'John Bull'. Hu established, among other regulations, that a Gorsedd or Assembly of Druids and Bards must be held on an open, uncovered grass space, in a conspicuous place, in full view and hearing of all the people.

Concerning the educational facilities available to the so-called barbarous people of these islands, there were at the time of the Roman invasion forty Druidic centres of learning which were also the capitals of the forty tribes; of these forty known centres nine have entirely disappeared. These forty colleges were each presided over by a Chief Druid.[9] There were also in Britain three Archdruids, whose seats were at York, London and Caerleon-on-Usk.

The territories of the forty tribes (the original of our modern counties) preserve for the most part the ancient tribal limits. Yorkshire, for instance, retains the same disproportionate magnitude to our other counties—the territory of the large and powerful tribe, the Brigantes.

The students at these colleges numbered at times sixty thousand of the youth and young nobility of Britain and Gaul. Caesar comments on the fact that the Gauls sent their youth to Britain to be educated. One notable instance has been mentioned by J. O. Kinnaman, D.D., in his work on Archaeology: 'Pilate was not a Roman by nationality, but by citizenship. He was born a Spaniard and educated in Spain as far as the schools of that country could take him. Then he went to Britain to study in the universities of that country under the administration of the Druids. How long he studied in England is not now known; it was Pilate's ambition to become a Roman lawyer and the future governor of Palestine studied long enough in Britain to achieve not only this ambition but to absorb the Druidic philosophy rather than the Greek and Roman. *Vide* Pilate's question to our Lord as they were walking out of the Praetorium, ' "What is

Truth?",[10] this was a question which the Druids were ever accustomed to debate.'[11]

It required twenty years to master the complete circle of Druidic knowledge. Natural philosophy, astronomy, mathematics, geometry, medicine, jurisprudence, poetry and oratory were all proposed and taught—natural philosophy and astronomy with severe exactitude.[12]

Caesar says of the Druids: 'They hold aloof from war and do not pay war taxes; they are excused from military service and exempt from all liabilities. Tempted by these great advantages, many young men assemble of their own motion to receive their training, many are sent by parents and relatives. Report says that in the schools of the Druids they learn by heart a great number of verses, and therefore some persons remain twenty years under training.[13] They do not think it proper to commit these utterances to writing, although in almost all other matters, and in their public and private accounts they make use of Greek characters. I believe that they have adopted the practice for two reasons—that they do not wish the rule to become common property, nor those who learn the rule to rely on writing, and so neglect the cultivation of the memory; and, in fact, it does usually happen that the assistance of writing tends to relax the diligence of the student and the action of memory. . . . They also lecture on the stars in their motion, the magnitude of the earth and its divisions, on natural history, on the power and government of God; and instruct the youth on these subjects.'[14]

While the Druids used writing for all other subjects taught in their colleges, they never used this medium in connection with the subject of religion. To the spread of Christianity we owe most of the information we possess of the Druidic religion; their secret laws gradually relaxed as they became Christian, and some of their theology was then committed to writing.

Dr. Henry, in his *History of England,* has observed that collegiate or monastic institutions existed among the Druids.[15]

Caesar several times calls the Druidic institution a *disciplina,*[16] a term that implies a corporate life—organization as well as the possession of learning. Mela speaks of the Druids as 'teachers of wisdom'.[17] The affirmation of Diodorus that 'some whom they call Druids, are very highly honoured as philosophers and theologians' is repeated by Hippolytus.[18]

Not only the supreme king, but every other king had his Druid and Bard attached to his court. This Druidic chaplain had charge of the education of the youthful members of the house, but was also allowed to have other pupils. He taught and lectured on all appropriate occasions, often out-of-doors, and when travelling through the territory of his chief, or from one territory to another, his pupils accompanied him, still receiving instruction; when, however, the pupils exceeded in number that which he was entitled by law on such occasions to have accommodated as his own company at a house, those in excess were almost always freely entertained by neighbours in the locality.

The chief poet seems to have been always accompanied by a number of assistants of various degrees, who had not yet arrived at the highest attainment of their profession.[19]

The theological students were given a particularly long course of training, and no Druidic priest could be ordained until he had passed three examinations in three successive years before the Druidic college of his tribe. The head of the clan possessed a veto on every ordination.[20]

By very stringent laws the number of priests was regulated in proportion to the population; and none could be a candidate for the priesthood who could not in the previous May Congress of the tribe prove his descent from nine successive generations of free forefathers. Genealogies, therefore, were guarded with the greatest care. This barrier to promiscuous admission had the effect of closing the Order almost entirely to all but the Blaenorion or aristocracy, making it literally a 'Royal Priesthood'.

Degrees were conferred after three, six and nine years training. The highest degree, that of Pencerdd or Athro (Doctor of Learning), was conferred after nine years. All degrees were given by the king or in his presence, or by his license before a deputy, at the end of every three years.[21]

Druidic physicians were skilled in the treatment of the sick; their practice was far removed from the medicine-man cult, so unfairly ascribed to them by their contemporary enemies, and lightly followed ever since. They prayed to God to grant a blessing on His gifts, conscious that it should always be remembered that no medicine could be effective nor any physician successful without Divine help. The chief care of the physicians was to prevent rather than to cure disease. Their recipe for health was cheerfulness, temperance and exercise.[22] Certainly the power of physical endurance displayed by the early Britons was a strong testimony to the salutary laws of hygiene enforced and the general mode of life encouraged by the Druids.

Human bones which had been fractured and re-set by art have been found in Druidic tumuli.[23]

Astronomers were deeply versed in every detail of their profession; such classic judges of eminence as Cicero and Caesar, Pliny and Tacitus, Diodorus Siculus and Strabo, speak in high terms of the Druid astronomers.

Strabo has left us a vivid description of the dress of the Britons of his day. On the visit to Athens of the British Druid astronomer, Abaris (Hebrew Rabbi), the Greek geographer writes: 'He came not clad in skins like a Scythian, but with a bow in his hand, a quiver hanging on his shoulders, a plaid wrapped about his body, a gilded belt encircling his loins, and trousers reaching down from the waist to the soles of his feet. He was easy in his address; agreeable in his conversation; active in his dispatch and secret in his management of great affairs; quick in judging of present accuracies, and ready to take his part in any sudden emergency; provident withal in guarding against futurity; diligent in the quest of wisdom; fond of friendship; trusting very little to fortune, yet having the entire confidence of others, and trusted with everything for his prudence. He spoke Greek with a fluency that you would have thought that he had been bred up in the Lyceum; and conversed all his life with the academy of Athens.' This visit of the British Druid was long remembered at Athens. Abaris travelled extensively in Greece; Greek fancy transformed the magnetic needle by which he guided his travels into an arrow of Apollo which would transport him at wish whithersoever he pleased.[24]

Ammianus Marcellus, A.D. 350, says, 'The Druids are men of penetrating and subtle spirit, and acquired the highest renown by their speculations, which were at once subtle and profound.'[25] Pomponius Mela[26] plainly intimates that the Druids were conversant with the most sublime speculations in geometry and in measuring the magnitude of the earth.

Stonehenge, 'the Greenwich Observatory' and great solar clock of ancient times, was pre-eminently an astronomical circle. Heliograph and beacon were both used by the ancient British astronomer in signalling the time and the seasons, the result of observations, for the daily direction of the agriculturist and the trader.

The unit of measure employed in the erection of Stonehenge, and all other works of this nature in our islands, was the cubit, the same as used in the Great Pyramid.[27]

The supposed magic of the Druids consisted in a more thorough knowledge of some of the sciences than was common.— astronomy, for instance. Diodorus Siculus states that the Druids used telescopes[28]—this evidently is the origin of the story that the Druids could by magic bring the moon down to the earth.

Many of the wells on Druidic sites, known today as holy wells, were the old telescope wells of the Druids, connected with their astronomical observations.[29] The old saying, 'Truth lies at the bottom of a well', comes down to us from those ancient times.

British architects trained in Druidic colleges were in great demand on the Continent. In this country the profession of architect was legally recognized. There were three offices of Chief Architect,[30] the holders of which were privileged to go anywhere without restriction throughout the country, provided they did not go unlawfully.

James Ferguson, the writer of one of our best histories of architecture, says : 'The true glory of the Celt in Europe is his artistic eminence, and it is not too much to assert that without his intervention we should not have possessed in modern times a church worthy of admiration, or a picture, or a statue we could look at without shame, and, had the Celts not had their arts nipped in the bud by circumstances over which they had no control, we might have seen something that would have shamed even Greece and wholly eclipsed the arts of Rome. . . . The Celts never lived sufficiently long apart from other races to develop a distinct form of nationality, or to create either a literature or a policy by which they could be certainly recognized; they mixed freely with the people among whom they settled and adopted their manners and customs.'[31]

C. J. Solinus, the Roman geographer, in his description of Britain, mentions the hot springs of Bath, and the magnificence with which the baths at that place had already been decorated for the use of bathers.[32]

The primitive religion of Britain associated in so many minds with the worship of the heavenly bodies, was the worship of the 'Lord of Hosts', the Creator of the Great Lights, the sun and moon, not the worship of the heavenly bodies themselves. The Universe was the Bible of the ancients, the only revelation of the Deity vouchsafed them. The wonders of nature were to them as the voice of the All-Father, and by the movement of the heavenly bodies they ordered their lives, fixed religious festivals and all agricultural proceedings.

The way to Christianity for the early inhabitants of Britain was traced by Nature herself, and from Nature to Nature's God. St. Paul, in his letter to the Corinthians, writes, 'Howbeit that was not first which is spiritual, but that which is natural; and afterward that which is spiritual.'

Strabo observes that the care of worshipping the Supreme Being is great among the British nation; and the history of Hume records that no religion ever swayed the minds of men like the Druidic.[33]

It has been said that the Druidic Circles cannot, in strictness, be termed temples, for the Druids taught that there were but two habitations of the Deity—the soul, the invisible—the universe, the visible. The word 'temple', in its primitive meaning, is simply a place cut off, enclosed, dedicated to sacred use, whether a circle of stones, a field or a building. In the old British language a temple or sanctuary was called a 'caer', a sacred fenced enclosure. The stone circles or caers of Britain were, therefore, essentially temples and held so sacred by the people that reverent behaviour in their vicinity was universal. Joshua, it will be remembered, by God's command, erected a circle at Gilgal (circle) immediately upon the arrival of the Chosen People in the Promised Land. The British caer has no connection with *castra*.

There seems, however, to be no doubt that generally the chambered barrows and cairns of Britain were used as temples; several points in their construction lead to this assumption. Mr. MacRitchie, in his *Testimony of Tradition*, mentions several of these points, among them fireplaces and flues for carrying away smoke.

Sir Norman Lockyer[34] states: 'Mr. Spence has pointed out the extreme improbability of Maeshowe (Orkney) being anything but a temple and, I may now add, on the Semitic model. There were a large central hall and side-rooms for sleeping, a stone door which could have been opened or shut from the inside, and a niche for a guard, janitor or hall porter.'[35]

The great circle and temple known as Avebury ('Ambresbiri, the Holy Anointed Ones') is of special interest as the Westminster Abbey of ancient times,[36] the last resting-place of princes, priests and statesmen, warriors, poets and musicians. One of the old Druids alluding to Avebury calls it 'The Great Sanctuary of the Dominion'.[37]

The Circles or temples were composed of monoliths upon which the employment of metal for any purpose was not permitted. Druidic worship was without figure or sculpture of any kind.[38] The monolithic avenues, symbolic of the sun's path through the Zodiac, were in some instances seven miles long. The national religious procession moved through these to the circle on the three great festivals of the year. In several of our own cathedrals we have the signs of the Zodiac, represented as sacred emblems on the tiles of the sanctuary floor, for instance at Canterbury and Rochester.

In his description of the temple at Jerusalem, Josephus states: 'The loaves on the table, twelve in number, symbolized the circle of the Zodiac.'[39]

Druidic services were held while the sun was above the horizon; the performing of ceremonies at any other time was forbidden by law.[40] The Chief Druid, or the Archdruid when he was present, occupied a position by a large central stone, approaching it with a sword carried by its point to signify his own readiness to suffer in the cause of 'truth.[41] This central stone called Maen Llog, or the Stone of the Covenant, and now distinguished by the name of Cromlech, was in Ireland called 'Bethel'[42] or the house of God. Near to it was another, which received in a cavity water direct from the clouds. This water, and the waters of the river Dee (called Drydwy, the Divine water), the Jordan of ancient Britain, were the only waters permitted to be used in Druidic sacrifices.

In the 'Faerie Queen' Spenser speaks of the:

> '... Dee which Britons long ygone
> Did call divine, that doth by Chester tend.'

For centuries after Druidism had merged into Christianity the Dee continued to be regarded as a sacred river. A striking instance of folk-memory is recorded in connection with the Battle of Britain, A.D. 613, when Dionoth, Abbot of Bangor, delivered an oration to the defeated Britons (who had retreated along the banks of the river), and concluded by ordering the soldiers to kiss the ground in commemoration of the body of Christ, and to take up the water in their hands out of the river Dee and drink it in remembrance of His sacred blood. This act gave the men fresh courage; they met the Saxons bravely, and Ethelfrid, the Northumbrian invader, was defeated.[43]

The Bards of Britain, whose office it was to cultivate the art of music and poetry as well as literature, are referred to by Strabo as hymn-makers;[44] they were responsible for the temple music and for the conduct of the musical part of the temple services. On these occasions they wore white robes—from this custom has descended our English Church custom of clothing the choristers in white surplices.[45]

It was not until the first century A.D. that the Jews introduced the wearing of surplices into their services. Josephus states : 'Now as many of the Levites as were singers of hymns persuaded the king (Agrippa) to assemble a Sanhedrin and to give them leave to wear linen garments as well as the priests; for, they said, this would be a work worthy of the times of his government, that he might have a memorial of such a novelty as being his doing; nor did they fail of obtaining their desire.'[46]

Referring to Stonehenge, Hecataeus, a Greek writer, 320 B.C., says that the people living in these islands worshipped in a beautiful temple, whose minstrels hymned with their golden harps[47] the praise of the God they adored, and whose priesthood was a regular descent from father to son.

While every British subject was entitled at birth to five British (ten English) acres of land for a home in the hereditary county of his clan, priests were entitled to ten acres (twenty English),[48] exemption from combative military service, permission to pass unmolested from one district to another in time of war, maintenance when absent on duty from their home, and contribution from every plough in their district.

The ceremonial dress of the Archdruid was extremely gorgeous, no metal but gold being used on any part of it. The Cymric Cross was wrought in gold down the length of the back of the robe; he wore a gold tiara and a breastplate of the same precious metal.[49] A breastplate was found in an excavated cist at Stonehenge, on the skeleton of an important Briton.[50] Five similar breastplates have been found in Britain and Ireland.

The Chevron Bead, a bead encased in gold, was worn by the Archdruid as a symbol of the Deity[51] and designated by the Roman historians the 'Druid's Egg', around which so much legend has been woven by the imaginative uninformed, who saw in the symbol only a talisman endowed with most magical powers.

The stories that are told and believed of human sacrifice by the Druids are pure inventions of the Romans to cover their own cruelty and to excuse it. The Druids sacrified sheep, oxen, deer and goats; charred remains of these have been found at Avebury,

Stonehenge and in the vicinity of St. Paul's Cathedral. No trace of human sacrifice has been discovered in Britain.[52]

It is very generally believed that the Celts were nature worshippers, that they gave Divine honours to rivers, mountains and woods. It is entirely a mistake to believe that they did so. They were nature lovers— never nature worshippers; neither had they a multitude of gods and goddesses, as is often affirmed. The gods and goddesses were mere mascots, and even to their descendants[53] mascots and charms have lost none of their popularity.

Other nations never obtained a proper comprehension of Druidism; they corrupted what they had learned of the Druidism of Britain, blending with it religions less pure. It is recorded by Caesar that those in Gaul who wished to be perfectly instructed in Druidism crossed the sea to what they believed to be its birthplace.

In the Christian era St. Patrick used the shamrock to instruct the people in the doctrine of the Trinity, and in earlier days the Druids used the oak for the same purpose. They sought a tree having two principal arms springing laterally from the upright stem, roughly in the form of a cross. Upon the right branch they cut the name Hesus; upon the middle or upright stem Taranis; upon the left branch Belenis; over this they cut the name of God—Thau.[54] The Hebrew prophets, it will be noted, referred to their expected Messiah as 'The Branch'.

The mistletoe was another form of representation to them of their Hesus, to whose coming they looked forward with as great expectancy as did the Jews in the East to their Messiah—the Britons were actually in advance of the Jews, for while the Britons believed in the resurrection of the body, many of the Jews did not.

'The Druids', writes Caesar, 54 B.C., 'make the immortality of the soul the basis of all their teaching, holding it to be the principal incentive and reason for a virtuous life.'[55]

The similarity of the Semitic and British forms of worship has been commented upon by archaeologists and others who have explored megalithic remains in this country. Sir Norman Lockyer states: 'I confess I am amazed at the similarities we have come across';[56] and Edward Davies: 'I must confess that I have not been the first in representing the Druidical as having had some connection with the patriarchal religion.'[57] William Stukeley, from a close study of the evidence affirms: 'I plainly discerned the religion professed by the ancient Britons was the simple patriarchal religion'[58]—an opinion which every critical and candid student of Druid ritual, customs, and teaching must endorse.

The unity of the Godhead was the very soul and centre of Druidism, and this unity was a Trinity. Procopius of Caesarea, A.D. 530, states: 'Jesus, Taran, Bel—One only God. All Druids acknowledge one Lord God alone.'[59]

The indisputable fact is that the Druids proclaimed to the universe, 'The Lord our God is One.' When Christianity preached Jesus as God Druidism had the most familiar name of its own Deity presented to it.

In the ancient British tongue Jesus had never assumed its Greek, Latin or Hebrew form, but remains the pure Druidic Yesu. It is singular that the ancient Briton never changed the name of the God he and his forefathers worshipped, nor has he ever worshipped but one God.[60]

In the Cornish folk-lore whole sentences were treasured up (without being understood), and when written down were found to be pure Hebrew. Three of these rendered into English are: 'Lift up your heads, O ye gates, and be ye lift up ye everlasting doors, and the King of Glory shall come in'; 'Who is this King of Glory?'; 'The Lord Yesu, He is the King of Glory.'[61]

Druidism with its self-evident Old Covenant origin, which latter was, indeed, the great 'oral secret' transmitted by Druid sages from generation to generation, its doctrine of the Trinity, worship entirely free from idolatry, furtherance of peace and contribution to the settling of disputes among the laity, high moral tone, and insistence on the liberty and rights of the subject, was a perfect preparation for the reception of Christianity.

Upon the introduction of Christianity the Druids were called upon, not so much to reverse their ancient faith, as to 'lay it down for a fuller and more perfect revelation'. No country can show a more rapid, natural merging of a native religion into Christianity than that which was witnessed in Britain in the first century A.D. The readiness with which the Druids accepted Christianity, the facilities with which their places of worship and colleges were turned to Christian uses, the willingness of the people to accept the new religion are facts which the modern historian has either overlooked or ignored.[62]

[1] Ed. Davies, *Celtic Researches*, pp. 171, 182.

[2] Diogenes Laertius in proem., p. 5. In proem., p. 6.

[3] Macpherson, *Dissertations*, p. 341.

[4] Gomer. A Brief Analysis of the Language and Knowledge of Ancient Cymry. London, 1854.

[5] Matthew Arnold, *Celtic Literature*, p. 254.

[6] Triodd Braint a Defod, Walter, op. cit. p. 33. Lloyds *History of Cambria*, ed. Powell, praef. p. 9.

[7] Myvy Arch., II, 57.

[8] *Traditional Annals of the Cymry*, p. 27. Triad H. Sharon Turner, *History Anglo Saxon*, Vol. I.

[9] *Gildas*, MS. (Julius, D.XI), Cottonian Library. Morgan's *British Cymry*.

[10] *John* 18 : 38.

[11] *Diggers for Facts*, pp. 226–229.

[12] Strabo, I, IV, p. 197. Caesars Comm. Lib. V. Sueotonius, V. Calegula. E. Campion, *Account of Ireland*, p. 18.

[13] See Toland's *History of the Druids*, p. 50.

[14] De Bell Gall. VII, 15, 16.

[15] Vol. I, Chap. II, p. 142, Amm. Marcel, *History*; IV, 9.

[16] De Bell Gall, VI, 13, 14.

[17] Pompon Mela, III, 2, 18.

[18] Philosoph, I.

[19] O'Curry's *Manners and Customs of Anc. Irish*, Vol. II. School of Simon Druid on O'Mulconry's Glossary: M.S.H. 2, 16 (Coll. 116), in Trinity College Library, Dublin. See also Reeve's *Adamnan*, p. 48.

[20] Stanihurst, *De Rebus in Hibernia*, p. 37.

[21] *Book of Lecain*, folio 168. Toland, *History Druids*, p. 223.

[22] J. Smith, *Gal. Antiq.*, p. 80.

[23] S. Lysons, *Our British Ancestors*, p. 44.

[24] Hecat. ab. Diod. Sicul, Lib. III. Avienus, *The Britannia*. Smith, *History of the Druids*, pp. 69, 70. Cartes, *History England*, Vol. I, p. 52.

[25] See note 3, p. 35.

[26] Lib. III.

[27] *Vide* Sir Norman Lockyer, *Stonehenge*, 1906.

[28] Wm. Stukeley, *Stonehenge*, p. 11.

[29] Strabo, Bk. XVII, Chap. I, Sir G. Cornwall. Lewis *Ast. of the Ancients*, p. 198.

[30] Triad, 32.

[31] *History of Architecture*, p. 73.

[32] *Monumenta Historica Britannica*, p. 12.

[33] *History of England*, Vol. I, p. 6.

[34] *Stonehenge*, p. 254.

[35] *Standing Stones and Maeshowe of Stennes*, 1894.

[36] Stukeley, *Abury*, p. 40.

[37] P. Lloyd, *Island of Mona*, p. 41.

[38] Origen on *Ezekiel*, Homily IV.

[39] Josephus, *Jewish Wars*, Bk. V, p. 132.

[40] Myo. Arch., Vol. III (Laws of Dynwal Moelmud).

[41] Ibid.

[42] Vallancy, *Collectanea de Rebus Hibernicus*, p. 211. Lysons, *Our British Ancestors*, p. 196.

[43] King's *Vale Royal*, p. 2. Annales Cambriae, CLXIX.

[44] Strabo, *Geogr.*, IV, 4, 5; XV, 1, 5. M. F. Cusack, *History of Ireland*, p. 116, note.

[45] E. Wilson, *Lights and Shadows*, p. 262. Triad, 233.

[46] Josephus, Antiq., Bk. XX, p. 9.

[47] Dio. Sic. Tom. I, p. 158. Taliesen, *Bards and Druids of Britain*, Nash, p. 15.

[48] *Ancient Laws of Cambria* (British Museum).

[49] Crania Britannicae, Vol. I, p. 78.

[50] Ibid.

[51] See E. Wilson's *Lights and Shadows*, pp. 6, 7.

[52] Hulbert's *Religions of Britain*, p. 37. Hen. Huntingdon History, Lib. III, apud res Anglia Script, p. 322, ed. Saville. Lewis, *History of Britain*, Ch. II.

[53] See Stukeley, *Abury*, pp. 2, 38, 49, 76.

[54] Schedius, *Treatise de Mor. Germ.*, XXIV. Thomas Maurice, *Indian Antiquities*, Vol. VI, p. 49.

[55] De Bell. Gall. Lib., VI, Chap. XIII.

[56] *Stonehenge and other British Monuments*, p. 252.

[57] *Mythology and Rites of the British Druids as ascertained from National Documents*, Pref. p. vii.

[58] *Abury*, Pref. p. i. G. Smith, *Religions of Ancient Britain*, p. 43.

[59] Origen on *Ezekiel*. (Richardson's *Godwin de Presulibis*.)

[60] Dr. Henry, *History of Great Britain*, I, 2.

[61] Rev. Dr. Margoliouth, *Jews in Britain*, Vol. I, p.23; Vol. III, p. 198.

[62] Rolleston, Mazzaroth, 113.

CHAPTER VI

IRISH DRUIDS

THE word 'Magi'—the Latin equivalent for 'Druids' —was used by early Irish writers and frequently by the Welsh; their synonymity in the modern mind appears to be almost entirely lost.[1]

The term 'Magi' conjures up a sacred meaning indicative of the exact opposite to that which we have been led to believe about the Druids.

'The Druids were, in Celtic Hagiology' constantly termed Magi.'[2]

It is quite possible that the 'Magi' of New Testament fame[3] who 'departed into their own country another way' (*Matt.* 2 : 12) visited Britain on their return journey to the East.

Tradition always bears a vein of truth; however fantastic, therein lies buried fact, and Irish historians have reiterated all along the centuries that Conor Macnessa, King of Ulster, who died A.D. 48, was made aware by his Chief Druid, Bacrach, of the happenings in Palestine at the time of the Crucifixion, this king, requiring of his Druid an explanation of the darkness that was 'over all the earth'[4] (*Luke* 23 : 44).

It is not improbable that the Druid had his information and enlightenment as to the fulfilment of prophecy from the visiting Druids or Magi from the East. It would be perfectly natural on the part of these Magi to visit Britain, the headquarters of Druidism.

James Heron, D.D., mentions 'a sacred caste in Ireland called Druida or Magi'.[5]

John Toland relates that in Ireland, as in England, the Druids were exempt from bearing arms, yet their decisions were final in matters concerning both peace and war; some of them were allied to kings, many of them were kings' sons, and great numbers were drawn from the aristocracy.

They wore long habits, as did the Bards and Ovates, but the Druids wore white surplices when they officiated in religious ceremonies. They, with the Bards and Ovates, had the privilege of wearing six colours in their breachans or robes; the king and queen, seven; lords and ladies, five; governors of fortresses, four; officers and young gentlemen, three; soldiers, two; and common people, one. This law, most of the Irish historians say, was enacted under Achaius (Eochaidh Ollamfodla) the First, a king of the Irish, 1383 B.C.[6]

This king also ordained that every noble person should have a coat of arms assigned to him to distinguish him in battle and to rally his followers, hence the crest. This cognizance was often appended to a man's name and became his surname.

The Bards were divided into three orders or degrees, namely, chronologers, heralds and poets. The first registered genealogies, the second sang the praises of great men, and the third, including inferior rhymers, lived most of the year free of cost.

In a great national assembly at Drumceat, in the

County Derry, under Aidus Ammireus, the eleventh Christian king, in the year 575, where were present Adius, King of Scotland, and St. Columba, it was decreed that for the better preservation of their history, genealogies, and the purity of their language, the supreme monarch and the subordinate kings with every lord of a cantred or hundred, should entertain a poet of his own, no more being allowed by the ancient law of the island, and that upon these and their posterity a portion of land should be settled for ever. At the Assembly St. Columba pleaded for the independence of Scottish Dalriada from Irish suzerainty, and for toleration for the Irish Bards, who had been banished by the king for their exactions and turbulence.[7] The inferior rhymers lived by travelling from place to place and by entertaining the people by satire and song.

It was also decreed that for the encouragement of poets and antiquaries, public schools should be appointed under the national inspection, and that the monarch's own bard should be arch-poet and have superintendence over the rest. With regard to public schools in Ireland, the Brehon Laws had distinct rules for the relation between pupil and teacher. The Brehon with his pupils constituted not a school in our sense of the term but a true family.[8] Ireland produced scholars of note. Fergil, known on the Continent as Virgilius the Geometer, affirmed the rotundity of the earth. Sedulius, eighth century, wrote on grammar, on government and on theology. Clement, an Irishman, was employed by Charlemagne along with

Alcuin and Dicuil, the author of a geography 'Liber de Mensura Terrae',[9] who was also Irish.

Writing in 1720 John Toland states: 'The Irish have incomparably more ancient material for their history than either the English or the French or any other European nation with whose manuscripts I have any acquaintance. In all conditions the Irish have been strangely solicitous, if not in some degree superstitious, about preserving their books and parchments, even those of them which were so as to be now partly unintelligible. Abundance through over-care have perished underground, the concealer not having skill for preserving them.'[10]

The most valuable pieces both in verse and prose were written by the Druids, some were interpolated after the prevailing of Christianity, which additions or alterations are, nevertheless, easily distinguishable. In these books were the rites and formularies of the Druids, together with their divinity and philosophy, and their two grand doctrines of the eternity and incorruptibility of the universe. Their laws were termed Celestial Judgments, and were only preserved in traditionary poems according to the institution of the Druids until committed to writing at the command of Conor Macnessa, King of Ulster, A.D. 48.

The three greatest encouragers of learning among the early Irish monarchy were King Achaius, 1383 B.C., surnamed the Doctor of Ireland, who is said to have built at Lothair Crofinn (Tara) an academy called 'The Court of the Learned'. It was he who ordained, for every principal family hereditary antiquaries, or in case of incapacity, the most able of the same historical house, with ranks and privileges after the Druids.

'The next promoter of letters was King Tuathalius, first century A.D., who appointed a triennial revision of all the antiquaries' books by a committee of three kings or great lords, three Druids and three antiquaries. These were to cause whatever was approved and found valuable in these books to be transcribed into the Royal Book of Tara.[11]

'The third patron of literature was King Cormac, A.D. 266, who renewed the laws about the antiquaries, and rebuilt and enlarged the academy of Tara for history, law and military training. He was an indefatigable distributor of justice, having written numerous laws still extant.[12]

'After the introduction of Christianity, the Druid, where he accepted the new religion, became bishop or priest, but great numbers remained on the same footing, insomuch that for a long time after the English conquest, the judges, bards, physicians and harpers held such tenures in Ireland.

'The O'Duvegans were hereditary bards; the O'Clerys and the O'Brodins were hereditary antiquaries; the O'Shiels and the O'Canvans were hereditary doctors; the Macglanchys were hereditary judges.

'The Druids did not at all times receive fair treatment from the Christians. Dudly Forbes, in a letter to an Irish writer, states that in St. Patrick's time no fewer than one hundred and thirty volumes relating to the affairs of the Druids were burnt in Ireland. What a deplorable extinction of arts and inventions; what an unspeakable detriment to learning. What a dis-honour upon human understanding has the cowardly proceeding of the ignorant, or rather the interested at all times occasioned.'[13]

Moore, the poet, when undertaking to write the history of Ireland, spoke slightingly of the value to the historian of Ireland, of the material afforded by national manuscripts. In the year 1839, Moore, in company with Dr. Petrie, visited the Royal Irish Academy and was shown a number of ancient books useful for historical research and reference. Moore, on briefly scanning these books, turned to Dr. Petrie and said, 'Petrie, these huge tomes could not have been written by fools or for any foolish purpose. I never knew anything about them before and I had no right to have undertaken the *History of Ireland.*' And from that day, Moore, it is said, lost all heart for going on with his *History of Ireland,* and it was only the importunity of the publishers which induced him to bring out the remaining volume.[14]

The bards survived the merging of Druidism into Christianity for centuries and enjoyed their ancient honours and privileges in many places down to the reign of Queen Elizabeth. Until 1746 the bards of Munster continued to hold their half-yearly sessions in the County of Limerick.

As with bards, the judges survived the fall of the Druidical system. They had for successors and repre-sentatives those who, in English, are called Brehon (from the Celtic word 'breathamh') which means 'judge'.

Cusack says that the whole system of government

and legislation was patriarchal—indicative of an Eastern origin—and that in the Brehon laws, said to be the oldest code of laws in Europe, there are evidences which look very like a trace of Jewish tradition.[15]

Another writer affirms that the Brehon Code in parts is a re-publication of the Mosaic law which declared that the first-born of every creature, including the first-born of man, was to be presented to the Lord (*Exod.* 13 : 2; *Num.* 18 : 15).[16]

In this connection it is interesting to note that the Welsh call the Irish Iddew and the country Iddewan or Jewsland.

Camden gives a quotation from Postellius' lecture on Pomponius Mela, a first-century writer: 'Ireland was then called Jurin, quasi Jewsland, because in the distant past the Jews (Israel), who were great soothsayers, knew that the future empire of the world would come to these parts.'[17]

The Psalter of Cashel says: 'The Tuatha de Danaan ruled in Ireland for about two centuries and were highly skilled in architecture and other arts from their long residence in Greece.'

Sir Henry Maine observed: 'We who are able here to examine coolly the ancient Irish law in an authentic form see that it is a very remarkable body of archaic law, unusually pure from its origin.'[18]

As in Britain, so in Ireland, human bones which had been fractured and re-set have been found in Druidical tumuli.

When Nuedha, an early Irish king, lost his hand in battle, 'Creidne, an artificer, put a silver hand upon

him, the fingers of which were capable of motion.'
Moreover, besides possessing ships and armies and
working in the metals, the Irish had an organized
body of surgeons, whose duty it was to attend upon
the wounded in battle; these were drawn from the
Druid class who preserved the history of the country
and the deeds of kings and heroes.[19]

[1] Rev. W. Hughes, *Church of the Cymry*, p. 4. Rev. D. James,
Patriarchal Religion, p. 19. Holinshed, *Chronicles*, p. 19.
Vallancy, *Collect de Rebus Herbernicus*, pp. 454–456. *Book
of Rights*, p. xlix. Adamnan, *Vita S. Columbae*, p. 73 (see also
Reeve's note to this word). Pliny, *Natural History*, XVI, 43, 95.
King Laehaire (fifth century) is described in the *Book of
Amagh*, fol. 3b as surrounded by his Magi.

[2] Rev. G. F. Maclear, D.D., *Conversion of the West. The
Celts*, p. 24.

[3] Book of Taliesen in Skene's *Four Ancient Books of Wales*,
Vol. II, p. 174. *Matt.* 2 : 1, "Feuch Tangedar Druids a Naird
shor go Hearulsalem" (Celtic). The advent was prophesied by
Cu Cullan the Irish High Priest or Archdruid (Archbishop
Cormac's Lexicon).

[4] Registered by the Pagan annalist Phlegon in his chronology
of the Olympiads, Bk. 13 under ol. 202–4.

[5] *The Celtic Church in Ireland*, p. 42.

[6] O'Curry, *Manners and Customs*, Vol. I, p. 244. C.
O'Connor, *Diss. on Irish History*, p. 6.

[7] Adamnan I, 11, 13 (Reeves). Montalembert, *Monks of the
West*, Vol. 3, p. 76.

[8] O'Curry, *Manners and Customs*, Vol. 2, p. 84.

[9] James Heron, D.D., *The Celtic Church in Ireland*, p. 212.

[10] *Libra Lintei*, registers written on linen mentioned by Livy,
44 B.C.

[11] Cusack, *Irish Nation*, p. 33.

[12] Lady Ferguson, *The Irish Before the Conquest*, p. 137.

[13] J. Toland, *History of the Druids*, pp. 82, 93.

[14] Matthew Arnold, *Celtic Literature*, p. 44.

[15] Cusack, *Irish Nation*, pp. 99–103.

[16] James Heron, D.D., *The Celtic Church in Ireland*, p. 175.

[17] *Britannic*, p. 963.

[18] *Early History of Institutions*, p. 19.

[19] Ignatius Donnelly, *Atlantis*, Lib. VI.

CHAPTER VII

ROMANS AND DRUIDISM

THE first decree against the Druids was enacted by the Emperor Tiberius under the plausible pretext of punishing them for offering human sacrifice—a decree as cruel as the pretext was false. The real reason was to destroy their influence in the state, an influence which extended through all the tribes.[1]

'When the Romans', observed Cleland, 'effected a footing in Britain they found in Druidism a constant and implacable enemy to their usurpation. They would have been glad to introduce their own religion, but to that point there was an invincible obstacle in the horror and contempt of the natives for a religion formed of their own allegories which made the name of the Roman gods as familiar to them as Julius Caesar states, but in a sense which excluded them from reception in a Divine one.'[2]

The report on the Druids as given by Suetonius Claudius and passed on to other Roman historians, accusing them of arranging for frightful holocausts of victims in wicker cages, has nothing but the assertion of this hostile Roman general to support it. The same historians accused the early Christians of 'abominable practices'.[3]

The Romans did indeed, themselves, on many occasions, burn the houses of the Britons, which were, in the case of the poorer inhabitants, made of wicker-work covered with clay.

Bishop Browne describes the work of an antiquarian who dug up one of these dome-shaped hillocks and found the remains of the old British houses of wicker-work, the impress of the wicker remaining on the burnt clay, as indelible as the writing upon Assyrian monuments.[4] The Roman story is a palpable invention to cover their own inhuman methods of warfare.

The Druidic religion, like the Christian religion, was diametrically opposed to all other religious practices in the world. Druidism and Christianity were both marked for destruction by the Romans. Athenagoras, A.D. 176, in his work entitled 'An Embassy' concerning the Christians, carefully describes and indignantly repudiates the three charges of atheism, cannibalism and lust, which were commonly urged against Christians in connection with their Eucharists, and pleads for an impartial trial that would lead to a just verdict.

In the case of Christianity, all efforts to bring it into opprobrium and to annihilation were overcome. It lived to vindicate its quality and to cover the world with its beneficent institutions and influence.

With Druidism the case was different, as at the very beginning of the Christian era it quickly dissolved as a separate organization. Druidism eagerly accepted a fuller revelation and became merged in Christianity. The immediate need, therefore, was not the defence of the principle and practice of the Druidic religion, but knowledge of a faith of which, hitherto, very little had been perpetuated in writing. Consequently real

Laegaire and all the provincial kings of Ireland, however, granted to every man free liberty of preaching and professing the Christian religion if he wished to do so.'[19]

The cumulative evidence of early historians leaves no shadow of doubt that Britain was one of the first, if not the first, country to receive the Gospel, and that the apostolic missionaries were instrumental in influencing the change whereby the native religion of Druidism merged into Christianity.[20]

It is a remarkable circumstance that while statues of gods and goddesses prevail throughout the heathen sites of Egyptian, Greek, Roman, Hindu and other idolatrous nations, not a vestige of an idol or image has been found in Britain.

If Mithraism is argued to contest this statement it should be observed that invaders were not free from idolatry. Mithra worship was a Roman importation. The British were entirely free from all forms of idolatry; they never adopted Mithraism.

The Druids' invocation was to one all-healing and all-saving power. Can we be surprised that they so readily embraced the gospel of Christ?

Further support for the early introduction of Christianity to Britain is gathered from the following widely diverse sources:

Eusebius of Ceasarea speaks of apostolic missions to Britain as matters of notoriety. 'The Apostles passed beyond the ocean to the isles called the Brittanic Isles.'[21]

Tertullius of Carthage, A.D. 208, the embodiment of the highest learning of that age, tells us that the

Christian Church in the second century extended to 'all the boundaries of Spain, and the different nations of Gaul and parts of Britain inaccessible to the Romans but subject to Christ.'[22]

Origen, in the third century, states: 'The power of our Lord is with those who in Britain are separated from our coasts.'[23]

'From India to Britain', writes St. Jerome, A.D. 378, 'all nations resound with the death and resurrection of Christ.'[24]

Arnobius, on the same subject, writes: 'So swiftly runs the word of God that within the space of a few years His word is concealed neither from the Indians in the East nor from the Britons in the West.'[25]

Chrysostom, Patriarch of Constantinople, A.D. 402, supplies evidence in these words: 'The British Isles which lie beyond the sea, and which lie in the ocean, have received the virtue of the Word. Churches are there found and altars erected. Though thou should'st go to the ocean, to the British Isles, there thou should'st hear all men everywhere discussing matters out of the Scriptures.'[26]

Gildas, the British historian, writing in A.D. 542, states: 'We certainly know that Christ, the True Sun, afforded His light, the knowledge of His precepts, to our Island in the last year of the reign of Tiberias Caesar, A.D. 37.'[27]

Sir Henry Spelman states, 'We have abundant evidence that this Britain of ours received the Faith, and that from the disciples of Christ Himself soon after the Crucifixion',[28] and Polydore Vergil observes that 'Britain was of all kingdoms the first that received the Gospel'.[29]

The fact that Lucius established Christianity as the State religion excludes the claim of the Latin Church to that eminence. That this early establishment was acknowledged beyond the confines of Britain is well expressed by Sabellius, A.D. 250. 'Christianity was privately expressed elsewhere, but the first nation that proclaimed it as their religion, and called itself Christian, after the name of Christ, was Britain';[30] and Ebrard remarks, 'The glory of Britain consists not only in this, that she was the first country which in a national capacity publicly professed herself Christian, but that she made this confession when the Roman Empire itself was pagan and a cruel persecutor of Christianity.'

The writer of *Vale Royal* states, 'The Christian faith and baptism came into Chester in the reign of Lucius, king of the Britons, probably from Cambria, *circa* A.D. 140.'[31]

Missionaries are said to have come from Glastonbury, only thirty miles distant, to instruct the Druids of Amesbury in the Christian faith. When the Druids adopted and preached Christianity, their universities were turned into Christian colleges and the Druid priests became Christian ministers; the transition was to them a natural one.

In the days of Giraldus Cambrensis (twelfth century), as a result of Roman Catholic doctrine, martyrdom and celibacy were much overrated, and it was thought a reproach to the Druids that none of their saints had 'cemented' the foundation of the Church with their blood, all of them being confessors, and not one gaining the crown of martyrdom.[32] An absurd charge, blaming the people for their reasonableness, moderation and humanity, and taxing the new converts for not provoking persecution in order to gain martyrdom.

It is not contended that every individual Druid and bard accepted Christianity on its first promulgation in Britain. Even after Christianity had become the national religion, petty kings, princes and the nobility retained, in many instances, Druids and bards. Druidism did not entirely cease until almost a thousand years after Christ.

Had the large collection of British archives and MSS. deposited at Verulum as late as A.D. 860 descended to our time, invaluable light would have been thrown on this as on many other subjects of native interest.

We read in an historical essay, 'The Ancient British Church', by the Rev. John Pryce, which was awarded the prize at the National Eisteddfod of 1876, these words: 'In this distant corner of the earth (Britain), cut off from the rest of the world, unfrequented except by merchants from the opposite coast of Gaul, a people who only conveyed to the Roman mind the idea of untamed fierceness was being prepared for the Lord.

'Forecasting the whole from the beginning and at length bringing the work to a head, the Divine Logos unveiled Himself to them in the person of Christ, as the realization of their searching instincts and the fulfilment of their highest hopes. It would be difficult to conceive of Christianity being preached to any people for the first time under more favourable conditions. There was hardly a feature in their national character in which it would not find a chord answering and vibrating to its touch.

'Theirs was not the sceptical mind of the Greek, nor the worn-out civilization of the Roman, which even Christianity failed to quicken into life, but a religious, impulsive imagination—children in feeling and knowledge, and therefore meet recipients of the good news of the kingdom of heaven.

'To a people whose sense of future existence was so absorbing that its presentiment was almost too deeply felt by them, the preaching of Jesus and the Resurrection would appeal with irresistible force.

There was no violent divorce between the new teaching and that of their own Druids, nor were they called upon so much to reverse their ancient faith as to lay it down for a fuller and more perfect revelation.'

Well has the Swedish poet, Tegner, in 'Frithiofs Saga', pictured the glimmerings of the dawn of Gospel day, when he described the old priest as prophesying :

'All hail, ye generations yet unborn
Than us far happier; ye shall one day drink
That cup of consolation, and behold
The torch of Truth illuminate the world,
Yet do not us despise; for we have sought
With earnest zeal and unaverted eye,
To catch one ray of that ethereal light,
Alfader still is one, and still the same;
But many are his messengers Divine.'

1 Rev. T. McLauchlan, *The Early Scottish Church*, p. 431.
2 *Trias Thaumaturga*, p. 156b.
3 Freculphus apud Godwin, p. 10. See *Hist. Lit.*, II, 18.
4 Baronius add. ann. 306. Vatican MSS. Nova Legenda.
5 Domesday Survey Fol., p. 449.
6 See Epistolae ad Gregorium Papam.
7 See *Joseph of Arimathea*, by Rev. L. Smithett Lewis.
8 *Concilia*, Vol. I, p. 9.
9 *Malmes., History of the Kings*, pp. 19, 20.
10 G. Smith, *Religion of Ancient Britain*, Chap. II, p. 37.
11 Morgan, *St. Paul in Britain*, p. 73.
12 Nath. Bacon, *Laws and Government of England*, p. 3.
13 Baronius ad Ann 459, ex. Actis Marcelli.
14 Moncaeus Atrebas, *In Syntagma*, p. 38.
15 Nennius (ed. Giles), p. 164. Book of Llandau, pp. 26, 68, 289.
16 Morgan's *British Cymry*.
17 Ussher (ed. 1639), pp. 5, 7, 20.
18 *The Mysteries of Britain*, pp. 62, 64, 65.
19 Dudley Wright, *Druidism*, p. 12.
20 Holinshed, *Chronicles*, p. 23.
21 *De Demostratione Evangelii*, Lib. III.
22 *Adv. Judaeos*, Chap. VII. Def. Fidei, p. 179.
23 Origen, *Hom. VI in Lucae.*
24 *Hom. in Isaiah*, Chap. LIV and Epist. XIII ad Paulinum.
25 *Ad Psalm*, CXLV, III.
26 Chrysostom, *Orat O Theo Xristos.*
27 *De Excidio Britanniae*, Sect. 8, p. 25.
28 *Concilia*, fol., p. 1.
29 Lib. II.
30 Sabell. Enno, Lib. VII, Chap. V.
31 King's *Vale Royal*, Bk. II, p. 25.
32 Topograph. Hibern Distinct. III, Cap. XXIX.

CHAPTER X

THE EARLY BRITISH CHURCH

THE name by which the British Church was first known in these islands was the Culdee Church, the natural result of Christianity having been introduced by the Culdich or 'refugees'. The ecclesiastics of this Church, composed chiefly of Christianized Druids, became known as the Culdees, and not until the Latin aggression, five centuries later, were they referred to as the British clergy in contradistinction to the clergy of the Roman Church. The fact is well established from the testimony of early writers and councils that through the Culdee church, the National Church of Britain is the Mother Church of Christendom.

The Culdees established Christian churches, monasteries and colleges, chiefly in remote places, where they fled from persecution by the Romans. Enlii (i.e. Bardsey), off the coast of Wales, once afforded shelter to twenty thousand Christians. Lindisfarne, Iona and many of the islands off the west coast of Scotland, and inaccessible parts of Ireland, were all inhabited in the early days of Christianity by the Culdees.

Eurgan, daughter of Caradoc and wife of Salog, Prince of old Sarum, founded a college of twelve Christian Druids (Culdee initiates) at Caer Urgan[1] or

Llantwit Major. This college must therefore have been established in the first century.

The Culdee Church was ruled by bishops[2] and elders — elder and priest (from presbyteros) being synonymous terms.[3] From an ancient authority we learn that the Culdees made no alteration in the terms used by the Druids; and they retained the white dress of the Druidic priests.[4] A superintendent among the Druids in Britain was a deon, i.e. a dean.

The clergy of the early Church came into office hereditarily; the principal of hereditary succession ran through the whole Celtic polity. The crown was hereditary with certain modifications peculiar to the Celts themselves. The bards were hereditary without much reference to qualification. In Ireland there was a hereditary succession in the bishopric of Armagh for fifteen generations.

Giraldus Cambrensis, Bishop of St. David's, in the twelfth century, a strong supporter of the Latin Church, complains of the Celtic Church that 'the sons after the deaths of their fathers, succeed to the ecclesiastical benefices, not by election, but by hereditary right'.[5]

Monasteries, or more correctly colleges, were attached to the early British Churches;[6] seats of learning were styled Cathair Culdich—the Chair of the Culdees.[7] The mode of life in these monasteries, however, was very different from that of the generality of those institutions that have been called monasteries in later ages. In each college there were twelve brethren, and one who was 'provost' or 'abbot'; wherever the Culdees formed a new settlement or college of presbyters, the fixed number of the council was twelve, following the example of the apostles of Jesus Christ.

Gildas states that in old phraseology—*sanctorum speluncae*—the monasteries, were the caves of the saints;[8] this makes intelligible the old records of the Culdees that they lived in kells or caves in Britain. Kings and nobility frequently passed their declining years in the peace and seclusion of these monasteries.

According to Jamieson there is a general tradition in the Highlands of Scotland that the Culdees immediately succeeded the Druids as the ministers of religion.[9] The tradition is supported by a circumstance of an interesting nature, which has been mentioned by several writers, that 'Clachan', the name still given in the Highlands to a place where a church stands, belonged originally to a Druidical temple. Hence it is still said, 'Will you go to the stones?' or 'Have you been to the stones?'; that is, 'Will you go to church' or 'Have you been to church?' At the end of the seventeenth century there was in a Highland parish of Scotland an old man who, although very regular in his devotions, never addressed the Supreme Being by any other title than that of 'Archdruid', accounting every other derogatory to the Divine Majesty.[10]

Toland states that two Druids acted as tutors to the two daughters of Laegaire (Leary), the high king of Ireland, in whose reign St. Patrick conducted his great revival; that Ida and Ono, Lords of Roscommon, were Druids and that Ono presented his fortress of Imleach-Ono to St. Patrick who converted it into the religious house of Elphin, later an episcopal see; this writer also states that the Druidical college of Derry was converted into a Culdee monastery.[11]

Adamnan, the successor and biographer of St. Columba, states that Columba was wont to say of the Lord Jesus, 'Christ the Son of God is my Druid.'[12]

Every fragment of such evidence is valuable, inasmuch as it manifests the true character of the Druids, and indicates the esteem in which even their memory was held long after Druidism had ceased as the national religion and had become merged in Christianity.

Archdeacon Munro, who made a tour of the Western Isles in 1549, begins his narrative with the Isle of Man, 'which sometimes, as old historiographers say, was wont to be the seat first ordained by Fynan, king of Scotland, to the priests and the philosophers, called in Latin "Druids", in English "Culdees", which were the first teachers of religion in Albion.'[13]

The Culdee, or British Church flourished increasingly from the first to the seventh century; kings and rulers of provinces united in enriching the Church.

Sir James Dalrymple observes that the common practice of the Culdees was to dedicate their principal churches to the Trinity, and not to the Virgin or any saint.[14] Sometimes, however, churches were named after their living founders.[15]

An account of the simplicity of the mode of service in the early Christian Church is found in the writings of Justin Martyr. He says: 'We offer up prayers in common for ourselves, for the baptized person, and for all men. . . . Then there is brought to the presiding brother a loaf of bread and a cup of water and mixed wine; he takes it and offers praise and glory to the Father of all, through the name of the Son and the Holy Spirit, and returns thanks to Him at great length for having vouchsafed to give us these things. When he has made an end of the prayers and the thanksgiving the people answer "Amen", which in Hebrew signifies "So be it". Then those whom we call deacons give to each person present a portion of the bread, wine and water, over which the thanksgiving has been said; and they also carry away to the absent. This food we call the Eucharist which no one may receive except those who believe in the truth of our doctrines, and who have also been baptized for the remission of sins and who live according to the commandments of Christ.' Later, in a communication to the Emperor, this ancient writer states: 'On Sunday, as the day is called, the inhabitants of town and country assemble together, and the memoirs of the Apostles and the writings of the Prophets are read as long as time permits. When the reader has finished, the presiding brother makes a discourse, exhorting us to an imitation of those worthies. Then we stand up and pray, and when the prayers are done, bread and wine are brought as I have just described; and he who presides sends up thanksgivings and prayers as well, and the people answer "Amen".'[16]

The early Christian missionaries did not seek a 'diseart' or place of retirement until their labours as active missionaries had come to an end; withdrawal from the world was not encouraged.

Writing of the early Church, Thomas Fuller 1608—

1661) says: 'Most of these men seem born under a travelling planet, seldom having their education in the place of their nativity; oft-times composed of Irish infancy, British breeding and French preferment; taking a cowl in one country, a crozier in another, and a grave in a third. Neither bred where born, nor beneficed where bred, but wandering in several kingdoms.'

These 'Wandering Scholars', as they were often termed, were learned in the classics as well as in Holy Writ. The Church continued to teach the classics; only for the Church the memory of them would have vanished from Europe. . . . The Church inherited the Roman respect for eloquence. 'The Holy writings do not teach the art of eloquence,' said Socrates, the historian, 'and by eloquence a man defends the truth.'[17] Clement I insists that 'secular learning is necessary to the right understanding of Holy Writ'.[18] Moses was learned in the wisdom of the Egyptians; Isaiah, the greatest of the prophets, was a gentleman and a scholar; St. Paul, the Apostle *par excellence,* was as versed in secular letters as afterwards in spiritual. It is to be remembered, however, that in spite of the greatness of the Vulgate its Latin prose is not such a masterpiece as the English of the Authorized Version'.[19]

Surprise is sometimes expressed that there are so few records of the early British Church. The savage edicts of Roman Emperors were directed not alone to the destruction of individuals who confessed the Christian faith, but also to the literature and records of the Church.

There were ten 'high power' persecutions of the Christians under these tyrants, extending from A.D. 66 to A.D. 303; the last being that of Diocletian which began in A.D. 290.[20] Bede says: 'The Diocletian persecution was carried out incessantly for ten years, with the burning of churches, outlawing of innocent persons and the slaughter of martyrs. At length it reached Britain in the year 300, and many persons, with the constancy of martyrs, died in the confession of the Faith.' The records of the Church had now to be written not with pen and ink but in blood and the flames of martyrdom. In the edict of Diocletian the Scriptures were to be carried away or destroyed, being regarded as books of magic; in this he was following older methods of suppression.

The British Church at this time lost the following by martyrdom: Amphibalus, Bishop of Llandaff; Alban of Verulam; Aaron and Julian, citizens and presbyters of Chester; Socrates, Bishop of York; Stephen, Bishop of London; Augulius, his successor; Nicholas, Bishop of Penrhyn (Glasgow); Melior, Bishop of Carlisle; and above ten thousand communicants in different grades of society.[21]

After the Diocletian persecution had died out, the churches in Britain were rebuilt,[22] and Christianity flourished to so great an extent that at the Council of Arles, A.D. 314, the British Church was represented by three bishops and a presbyter, and again at the Council of Sardica and Ardminium in the fourth century. It is interesting to note that the three bishops who represented the British Church at the Council of Arles came from York, London and Caerleon-on-

Usk,[23] the former seats of the three Archdruids of Britain.

Against the British Church no charge of heretical doctrine has at any time been made, though the very prince of heretics, Pelagius, was one of its most prominent and learned abbots.

The Pelagian heresy, originated by Morien,[24] better known by his Latin name, Pelagius, twentieth Abbot of Bangor-on-Dee, Flintshire, was nothing more than an attempted revival of Druidism, and of the old Druidic ideas with regard to the nature and free-will of man. The beauty of the Latin compositions of Pelagius, his extensive learning and reproachless life, facilitated the spread of the heresy everywhere; it was quickly suppressed in Britain.[25]

St. Hilary of Poictiers, in the latter part of the fourth century, wrote to the British Church : 'I congratulate you on having remained undefiled in the Lord, and untainted by all the contagion of damnable heresy. Oh, the unshaken steadfastness of your glorious conscience! Oh, house firm on the foundation of the faithful rock. Oh, the constancy of your uncontaminated will.'[26]

During the storm which the Pelagian heresy caused in Britain, one of the brightest lights of the Culdee Church, St. Patrick, was, in the providence of God, being prepared for his great work of revival among the Irish people, Christianity, according to Gildas, having been planted in Ireland before the defeat of Boudicca, A.D. 61.

Maelgwyn, or Patrick, the Apostle of Ireland and of the Isle of Man, born at Llantwit Major,

Glamorganshire, A.D. 363,[27] from whence he was taken prisoner and carried to Ireland, was, by tradition, a Culdee and the son-in-law of a bard;[28] by his own statement the son of a presbyter,[29] and grandson of a deacon, both of the British Church, St. Illtyds, Llantwit Major, to which was attached a college.[30]

Patrick's father, Calpurnius (not Patrick himself, as frequently erroneously stated), would appear to have been principal of this college, acting at the same time as an official of the Roman Empire, probably as broveratius, 'district justiciary and chief'. Patrick would, in such case, have early opportunity of acquiring a knowledge of Roman law and British Church government.

Niall of the Nine Hostages, so-called because five provinces in Ireland and four in Scotia delivered hostages to him, changed the name of North Britain from Albania to Scotia at the request of a colony of the Dalriada, the Irish colonists who had been led by Fergus from Antrim to Argyllshire. Niall, in one of his raids, took Patrick prisoner from Llantwit Major to Ireland in A.D. 379. The captive escaped to Gaul, returning to Ireland nearly fifty years later as a missionary revivalist.

St. Patrick is said to have introduced the use of the Latin language,[31] the previous missionaries having used chiefly Greek.[32] Latin, did not, however, rapidly supplant Greek. Professor H. Zimmer states: 'It is almost a truism to say that whoever knew Greek on the Continent in the days of Charles the Bald (tenth century), was an Irishman or was taught by an Irishman.'[33]

Bede does not mention Patrick for the very obvious reason that the Culdee hierarchy, with its hereditary succession, was obnoxious to Bede as an earnest adherent of the novel Papal Church introduced in A.D. 664, but he speaks of his contemporary, Palladius,[34] a Caledonian and a Culdee, who became like Ninian[35] an emissary of the Roman See, which was now resolutely setting itself to grasp the sceptre of universal dominion in the Christian Church.

Baronius states: 'The bishops of Ireland were all schismatics, separated from the Church of Rome.'[36]

Many saints of the British Church were, at a later date, claimed by the Latin Church, and legends undeserving of the slightest credence grew around their names. Those who owed nothing to Rome in connection with their conversion, and who long struggled against her pretensions, were later claimed by the Latin Church as though they had been her most devoted adherents. This is especially noticeable in the case of St. Patrick, whose conversion was the result of training in a British home, who was all his life a Culdee, yet is now given the greatest prominence in Roman Catholic hagiology.

Deliberate confusion was created by the Papal Church between the Culdee St. Patrick of the fifth century and a later Patrick of the ninth century who, according to the 'Chronicles of Ireland', was, in the year 850, Abbot of Ireland, Confessor. For there were two Patricks, the first a very learned and godly man, the second an abbot, given to superstition and founder of the fabulous Purgatory, which goes in Ireland under the name of St. Patrick's Purgatory. During a

great rebellion in Ireland, Patrick the Abbot was
compelled to flee the country. He fled into Britain and
lies buried at Glastonbury. The Martyrology of Sarum
reports that in Ireland they kept the feast of Patrick
the Abbot on the 24th of August.[37] It was to this
second Patrick that the Pope sent the pallium as a
reward for his Romanizing zeal, its first appearance in
Ireland.

The great St. Columba, fourth in descent from
Niall of the Nine Hostages, born A.D. 522, about fifty
years after the death of St. Patrick, was associated
with the Culdee Church of Iona for thirty-two
years, where he arrived from Ireland with his twelve
disciples on Pentecost Eve in the year 565. We are
here given another instance of the faithfulness of the
Culdees to first foundations in the formation of a new
settlement.

'Many of the Continental monasteries owed their
foundations to Irish scholars. When St. Columba
turned his back on Derry with the lament that is
one of the loveliest of the ancient Irish poems, and
founded the monastery at Iona, it was but the beginning of a movement which brought so many scholars
to the Irish schools. But the claim of the Irish
schools is not so much in the intricate treasure of their
manuscripts, as in the other pattern which they wove
into the history of Europe. Bangor was where Columbanus learnt his lighter Greek metres and the secret of
his exquisite and melancholy prose.'[38]

The ancient service book of the Abbey of Bangor
is still extant in the Ambrosian Library at Milan: it
is entitled 'Antiphonary of Bangor'. The primitive

church was fundamentally monastic; there was no papal jurisdiction in the primitive church in Ireland.[39] 'There was episcopacy in the Church but it was not diocesan episcopacy.'[40]

In *The Primitive Church of St. Peter* a bold attempt has been made by the author to 'Vaticanize' antiquity.[41]

The island called Inis-nan-Druidneach (Isle of Druids), the native name for Iona, was the abode of Druids whose predecessors had fled there from Roman Imperial persecution.[42] That eventually St. Columba and his disciples settled down with these Druids is a matter of history. They built a monastery for their own accommodation, and then with his missionary disciples St. Columba turned his attention to Scotland where Culdee missionaries had already taken the Gospel.

Of St. Columba his friends tell of him that 'he was angelical in look, brilliant in speech, holy in work, clear in intellect and just in council'.

St. Columba did not recommend long fasts (any more than long faces), but would have the brethren eat every day, that they might be able to work and pray every day.

One of his disciples and successors, Baithen, was distinguished not only for his holy life but for his learning. 'Know', said a learned man of his time, 'that there is no one on this side of the Alps who is equal to him in knowledge of the Scriptures, and in the greatness of his learning.'[43] Montalembert said also: 'I do not compare the disciple with his master. Columba is not to be compared to philosophers and learned men, but with patriarchs and apostles.'[44]

'He (Columba) established the little kingdom of the Scots and set upon the throne the king—Aidan— whose lineal descendant today occupies the throne of Great Britain. Although only a presbyter, he reigned supreme over all the churches of his order. His power was absolute, and for many years after his death the Abbot and Culdees of Hyona [Iona] gained so much favour and esteem of the people that even in their cloistered retreats they were at the head of all civil as well as ecclesiastical matters.'[45]

Surrounded by the stormy Atlantic a more desolate abode could hardly be imagined than Iona, and were it not for the ruins of the monastery, and the graves of the Norse kings around it, the traveller would never guess that it had once been the resort of princes from distant lands and had echoed to the sound of prayers, psalms and anthems. For two hundred years Iona was the lighthouse for the western nations, whence missionaries went forth in all directions.

It is known that in Iona in ancient times a great collection of books was made, and it is an interesting fact of history that Fergus II of Scotland, who in his youth assisted Alaric the Goth at the sack of Rome, A.D. 410, brought away as part of the plunder some valuable 'geir'[46] and a chest of books which he afterwards presented to the monastery of Iona. This presentation was made 164 years before St. Columba's date—clear evidence that St. Columba's famous library was founded by the Druids.

Ænius Silvius, afterwards Pope Pius II, sent a legate to Scotland to ascertain if the lost books of

Livy should be found among them. At a later date
(1525) Master John Campbell, Treasurer to the King,
found five old books which then consisted of nothing
but broken leaves which were very difficult to read.
Boece says that 'the reading sounded more like the
eloquence of Salustius than of Livy'.[47]

Fergus II is not to be confused with Fergus Mac-
Earc, sixth century, who with his followers from
Ireland settled in Caledonia. Fergus II (grandson of
Ethodius, who was banished from Scotland and
received by the King of Denmark) succeeded in
recovering his birthright possessions and the crown of
Scotland.[48]

An acquaintance with our ecclesiastical history will
enable us to discover what we should naturally expect
to find—that the government of the ancient Church
of our land was the same as that of all other churches
planted by the apostles, with whom it was in full
communion.

[1] Iola MSS., p. 343.
[2] Tertullian terms Bishops "Presidents", De Corona, Milit.
III, 4 (A.D. 211).
[3] Cyprian in Ep. II, applies the term Levite to a Presbyter.
(A.D. 230.)
[4] McCallum, History of Culdees, pp. 158, 159.
[5] Book of Llandav, p. 279. Topograph. Hebern. Distinct, III,
Cap. XXIX.
[6] Dugdale, Monasticon, Vol. I, p. 2. D. McCallum, History
of Culdees, p. 159.
[7] Jamieson, History of Culdees, p. 35, note.
[8] De Ex. Brit., CC. XXXIII–XXXVI.
[9] James Macpherson, Fingal (Dissertation), p. 7. McCallum,
History of Culdees, pp. 158, 159.
[10] Jamieson's Culdees, p. 25.
[11] History of the Druids, pp. 86, 91.
[12] Reeves, Life of Columba, p. 74. Tara Hill, pp. 205, 208.
[13] Miscellanea Scotica, Vol. II, p. 133.

[14] *Historic Collections*, p. 121.

[15] F. E. Warren, *Liturgy and Ritual of the Celtic Church*, p. 55.

[16] Justin Martyr, *Apology for the Christians*. A.D. 140.

[17] Soc. History Eccles, III, 16.

[18] Clement I. Epist. 4, quoted by Gratean. Decret I, 37, C.14.

[19] See Helen Waddell, *The Wandering Scholars*, XI and XVI.

[20] Tillemont, Vol. IV, pp. 508 ff. Allard, *La Persecution de Diocletian*, pp. 40, 41.

[21] Haddon and Stubbs, Vol. I, p. 32. Zosomen, *History Eccles*, Vol. I, p. 6. Fuller, *Ch. History Britain*, Vol. I, p. 20.

[22] Gildas, *De Exced Brit.*, Sect. 10, p. 10.

[23] Mansi Conciliorum Nova et ampliss. Collectio II, p. 476 (new ed.). Eusebius on Secrates, V, 23. Concelio Compiled (1) J. Crabbe.

[24] Iolo MSS., pp. 42, 43.

[25] Rev. R. W. Morgan, *St. Paul in Britain*, p. 161.

[26] Hilar Pictav, *De Synodis*.

[27] See Fryer's *Llantwit Major*.

[28] Tirechan's *St. Patrick*.

[29] Styled "Presbyter" in *Book of Durrow*, Vit Reeves ed., p. 242.

[30] Cottonian MSS. Vespasian A, XIV, printed in Rees' *Cambro British Saints*.

[31] Scoll, *De Eccles Brit. Scotor History Fontibus*, p. 17. Haddan & Stubbs, *Councils*, Vol. I, p. 175, note. Tripartite Life of St. Patrick.

[32] Reeves, *Adamnan*, p. 354.

[33] *Celtic Church in Britain and Ireland*, p. 92.

[34] *Eccles. History*, Chap. XIII.

[35] *Vita Ninian* (Aibred), Cap. II, Bede II, 4, 5.

[36] *Ecclesiastical Annals*.

[37] Meredith Hanmer, A.D. 1571.

[38] Helen Waddell, *Wandering Scholars*, p. 33.

[39] See *The Celtic Church in Ireland*, by James Heron, D.D., pp. 162, 163.

[40] Skene's *Celtic Scotland*, Vol. II, Bk. II, Chap. II, p. 44.

[41] Rev. Luke Rivington.

[42] *Ency. Brit.* (eleventh edition), Vol. XIV, p. 727. Llwyd, *Isle of Mona*, p. 49.

[43] Fentan.

[44] *Monks of the West*, Vol. III, p. 93.

[45] Fiona McLeod, *Hist. of Iona*.

[46] Celtic for treasure, usually armour or rich clothes.

[47] Boece, *Scotorium Historiae*, ed. J. Bellenden, 1531, p. 252.

[48] Ibid.

CHAPTER XI

THE ANGLO-SAXON INVASION

THE Anglo-Saxon invasion, which resulted in the most important and complete of all the tribal settlements in Britain, took place between A.D. 446 and 501.

In these incursions the Jutes and Angles were the first to arrive, and the Angles being numerically the strongest constituent, gave their name in this country to the entire group, which on the Continent were known as Saxons.

Curiously enough a belief persists that the Anglo-Saxons on their first arrival in this country were entirely pagan and that their conception of the Deity was expressed in the worship of numerous gods of their own imaginative creation. The exponents of this belief urge, in support of it, that memorials of these gods still exist, as, for instance, in the names of the days of the week; they cite Odin in connection with Wednesday as an outstanding example. Belief supported on such ground does not hold a position that is uncontestable. Grimm says : 'Among old Saxon and all Teutonic nations Odin signifies Divinity'; Peterson likewise : 'Odin's name bears allusion to mind and thought and breathing; it is the quickening, creating Power; it denotes the all-pervading spiritual Godhead.'[1] Odin was, therefore, the Scandinavian name for the Infinite Being.[2]

Confusion on this point arose in the minds of historians, owing perhaps to the fact that Sigge, son of Fridulph, a pontiff prince of Azoff in the Crimea, 72 B.C., took the name of Odin when he assumed the leadership of the early Saxons, spiritually as well as temporally, and led them with magnetic instinct from Asgard to north-western Europe.[3] As the Gigla-Saga says, 'Sometimes a chief's name referred to the God he especially worshipped.'[4]

Snorre, in his *Heimskringla* or 'Home Chronicles', tells how Odin was a heroic prince in the Black Sea region, with twelve peers and a great people straitened for room and how he led them across Europe. Odin and his peers became heroes to the descendants of these early Saxons and as such passed into legend and song.[5]

The modern Germans claim a share in the legends and traditions that have accumulated around the name of Odin; that illustrious individual, however, belonged exclusively to the Sakian (Saxon) race, and was in no way connected ethnically with the Germans.[6]

With the Anglo-Saxons, as with the Britons, the king was the last resort of justice and the source of all honour and mercy; he was to be prayed for and revered of all men of their own will without command, and was the especial protector of all churches, of widows and of foreigners.[7]

The Anglo-Saxon invasion had the effect of gradually pushing the Celts to the west of England and south-west Scotland. When this occurred and the Archbishops of Caerleon-on-Usk, London and York,

saw all the churches in their jurisdiction lying level
with the ground, they fled with all the clergy that
remained after so great a destruction, to the coverts
of the woods in Wales, and to Cornwall.[8] From this
fact it is easily discernible how it came to pass that
the Culdee or British Church has been associated to
so great an extent with Wales and Southern Scotland.

It has been said of the British Church that it made
no effort to convert the Saxons to Christianity. In this
connection several facts stand out very clearly: the
Druidic religion had not yet died out in Britain and
the Saxons found sufficient similarity between their
own form of worship and that of ancient Britain to
permit them to unite under the ministrations of a
Druidic hierarchy,[9] deriving their religion, it may be
concluded, from the same patriarchal source as the
Druids.

The Druidic law of tithing was observed by the
Anglo-Saxons, as by the Britons; the laws of Edward
the Confessor speak of them as claimed by Augustine
and conceded by the king, Ethelbert.

The Saxons looked with suspicion on efforts to
convert them to Christianity by those whom they were
endeavouring to subjugate, and who, though worshippers of the Infinite Being, were still non-Christian
when, in 597, the Augustinian mission sent by Pope
Gregory to introduce the Latin form of Christianity,
reached these shores.

The British Church was not unaware of the errors
of Rome, for we have Columbanus, a saint (whom the
Roman Church has calmly annexed, as they have
St. Patrick, St. Columba and other saints of the

primitive Church), writing to Pope Boniface IV: 'Your Chair, O Pope, is defiled with heresy. Deadly errors have crept into it; it harbours horrors and impieties. Catholic? The true Catholicism you have lost. The orthodox and the true Catholics are they who have always zealously persevered in the true faith.'

The civil power of Rome being dead, the ecclesiastical power began to rise on its ruins; and there may have been a connection between the two processes. The loss of one sphere of power may have helped to impel an ambitious people, accustomed to universal dominion, to seek after another sphere of power. The ambition of Pope Gregory became that also of the priest and delegate Augustine, to see the world brought under the sway of the fast-developing kingdom of Papal Rome, and when, in one day, Augustine baptized 10,000 Saxons the news of these 'conversions' created great joy in Rome.

The immediate success achieved by Augustine in Kent so impressed Pope Gregory that he dispatched more missionaries and with them Church ornaments and vestments. Among these was the famous 'pallium'. This cloak, of ancient origin, the Roman emperors had been accustomed to present to anyone whom they wished to mark with special honour. When the Popes began to assume imperial authority and to covet all the worldly splendour of the Caesars, they adopted the practice of bestowing the 'pallium' on those whom they wished to elevate.

The arrival of the 'pallium' in England for Augustine, was a significant event. By favour of the

Saxon king, Ethelbert, the Roman Church was set up at Canterbury; it became the chief seat of episcopal authority and was the origin of the Church known today as the Church of England. It will be observed that the origin of the British Church and that of the Church of England are quite distinct, with an interval of 560 years, and that the theory that Britain owes her Christianity to Augustine is without foundation in fact.

The majority of the Saxons converted to Christianity in 597 soon gave evidence that their hearts were unchanged; they quickly fell away to their old religion. By 635 the Latin Church in Kent had become reduced to inactivity through continual hostilities between the Britons and Saxons, to be revived thirty years later when Roman teaching and practices were imposed on the British Church of Northumbria and to spread rapidly over the whole country.

There was already at Canterbury the British church built by St. Martin (traditionally the brother of St. Patrick's mother, Conessa), who founded also various churches in Scotland, i.e. Kilmartin, and later that of Tours with which he has been historically associated. In passing it should be noted that the British Church founded the churches of Gaul. The Archbishops of Treves were, according to the Tungrensian Chronicles, always supplied from Britain and, coming nearer Rome itself, St. Cadval, a British missionary, founded in A.D. 170 the Church at Tarentum, after whom the Church at Tarento is still named.

The year 597, memorable alike for the death of St. Columba and the arrival of Augustine, has other outstanding claims to notice. When Augustine came he found in the province of the Angles seven bishoprics and an archbishopric, all filled with most devout prelates, and a great number of abbeys.[10]

The testimony of many writers that the intrusion of an emissary of the Pope was resented and resisted by the British Church, is supported by facts of history.

At a council held shortly after Augustine's arrival he was told that they 'knew no other Master than Christ', that 'they liked not his new-fangled customs', and that they refused subjection.[11] Augustine angrily replied, 'If we may not preach the way of life to you, you shall at the hands of your enemies, undergo their vengeance.' At the second conference with Augustine the British Church was represented by seven of her prelates, and although Baronius had the assurance to pronounce these bishops guilty of schism, he allows their governments to have been regular, and their faith orthodox. Both Augustine and his successors, by making the submission of the Britons to their authority, as metropolitans, the primary article of communion, leave it beyond doubt that they were fully satisfied with the purity of their doctrine, if not with the canonical succession of their bishops.

The British Christians scorned the idea that identity in certain tenets and practices with Papal Rome constituted even the shadow of a title, on the part of Papal Rome, to their allegiance. It is then no matter for surprise that on their first meeting with the delegate from Rome they should proclaim with one voice, 'We have nothing to do with Rome; we know nothing of the Bishop of Rome in his new character of the

Pope; we are the British Church, the Archbishop of
which is accountable to God alone, having no superior
on earth.'

The Britons told Augustine they would not be
subject to him, nor allow him to pervert the ancient
laws of their Church. This was their resolution and
they were as good as their word, for they maintained
the liberty of their Church for five hundred years after
his time, and were the last of all the Churches of
Europe to give up their power to Rome.[12] This fact
cannot be set aside in an unprejudiced study of British
Church history: Rome found here a Church older
than herself, ramifications of which struck into the
very heart of the continent of Europe. The farther we
go back into British history, the clearer shines forth
in all our laws the fact that the British Crown, Church
and people were entirely independent of all foreign
authority.[13]

All our great legal writers concur on this point.
'The ancient British Church', writes Sir William
Blackstone, 'by whomsoever planted was a stranger to
the Bishop of Rome and all his pretended authorities.'[14]

The Christians of Britain could never understand
why the Church of Rome, because she professed
certain truths, should arrogate spiritual despotism
over all who held the same. When Augustine
demanded of Dionoth, Abbot of Bangor Iscoed, or
Bangor-on-Dee, that he acknowledge the authority of
the Bishop of Rome, the reply of the Briton was a
memorable one: 'We desire to love all men, but he
whom you call "Pope" is not entitled to style himself

the "father of fathers" and the only submission we can render him is that which we owe to every Christian.'[15]

Cadvan, Prince of Wales, A.D. 610, expresses himself thus to the Abbot of Bangor : 'All men may hold the same truths, yet no man can hereby be drawn into slavery to another. If the Cymry believed all that Rome believes, that would be as strong a reason for Rome obeying us, as for us to obey Rome. It suffices for us that we obey the Truth. If other men obey the Truth, are they therefore to become subject to us? Then were the Truth of Christ made slavery and not freedom.'[16]

Wilfrid, a clever young priest, who had been brought up in the school of Iona, but had afterwards travelled to Rome and had become fascinated by her customs and grandeur, threatened, in his long-drawn suit with the See of Canterbury, in 670, to appeal to Rome. The threat was received with laughter as a thing never before heard of in England.[17]

The British Church recognized the Scriptures alone for its rule of faith,[18] was subject to no other Church on earth, and firmly resisted the unwarranted intrusion of a Pope. For almost two centuries Britain had been free from the domination of Imperial Rome; this fact enabled the supporters of the British Church at this time to quote the second canon of the Council of Constantinople, held in A.D. 381, which ordained that the Churches that are without the Roman Empire should be governed by their ancient customs.[19] But the canon was not held sufficient by Augustine and his successors to justify the British Church in its contention.

Though the doctrinal controversies which divided British and Roman Churches may seem unimportant to us, they plainly show our original ecclesiastical independence, and the stubborn resistance of our Church fathers to papal pretensions to supremacy.[20]

Beyond all question, to the national Church of Britain belongs that pre-eminence which the old British Triads claimed for it of being 'primary in respect to Christianity'.

The most famous of the British monasteries at the coming of Augustine was the monastery of Bangor-on-Dee, Wales. Bishop Dionoth presided over a flourishing body of Christians (numbering some thousands) whose headquarters were at this monastery.[21] The youths there educated were trained in Christian doctrine and sent forth as missionaries and teachers. Bangor, like Iona, was renowned for its zeal in propagating Christianity abroad. The refusal of its bishop, Dionoth, to acknowledge the authority of the Pope was the first of a long series of denials of the authority of the Pope in Britain.[22]

At the Synod of Chester held in 601, there were present, besides Augustine and some of his followers, seven British bishops and many men of great learning from the monastery of Bangor-on-Dee. Augustine, at this Synod, suffered a second defeat; the general assembly spoke out against the encroachments of Rome. 'The Britons', they exclaimed, 'cannot submit either to the haughtiness of the Romans, or the tyranny of the Saxons.'[23]

Augustine did not live to take vengeance on these early protestors; it was left to his successor to lead the Saxons against them, and in the massacre of Bangor, A.D. 613, twelve hundred Christians perished.[24]

William of Malmesbury, A.D. 1143, describes the ruins of Bangor Abbey in his day as those of a city—the most extensive he had seen in the kingdom.[25] Two other foundations in Britain retained their superiority over all others of a later date, under every change of ruler till the Reformation—St. Albans and Glastonbury.

The next interference of papal Rome with British customs took place in A.D. 664, the excuse for this attempt being the correct date for the observance of Easter.

King Oswy of Northumbria, with his brother Oswald, was converted by missionaries from Iona while in exile for seventeen years in Scotland, during the reign of the rival king, Edwin. Oswy adhered, naturally, to the usages of the Culdee Church, having been taught by the Scots. His queen, daughter of Ethelbert, King of Kent, had been brought up to observe the Latin way of reckoning, and each year the strange anomaly occurred of the king and his followers observing one day and the queen observing another day for the Easter festival.

The queen's chaplain, Romanus, and Wilfrid, tutor to the princes, were priests of the Roman Church, and urged the acknowledgment of the Roman calculation for Easter as being correct. At last the king resolved that the whole question would be debated and settled once and for all at the Synod of Whitby.[26]

Bishop Colman (Culdee Church of Northumbria) pleaded the British cause as having been derived from his forefathers, and originating in the teaching of St. John. Wilfrid, a cleverer man, was on the papal side and ridiculed British custom as compared with that of the Apostle 'to whom Christ had given the keys of heaven'. The king, eager to learn the truth, inquired further into this statement. Colman, simple-minded and honest, admitted that these words applied to St. Peter. The king then asked Wilfrid whether Christ had really given the keys of authority to Peter. Wilfrid answered in the affirmative, whereupon the king decided in favour of the papal party. Colman resigned his bishopric, and with many of his clergy went back to Iona, from which monastery he had come to Northumbria, and where the ancient British Easter continued to be observed for many years.

From the day of the historic Synod of Whitby the province ruled by Oswy agreed to observe Easter the Latin way; and the British Church, though proved to be the oldest national Church in the world, as confirmed by the Councils of Arles, Basle, Pisa, Constance and Sienna, was more and more coerced into conforming to papal customs and claims. For a time there were in Britain two Churches—the old British and the new Roman.

At the Council of Hertford, A.D. 673, only nine years after the Synod of Whitby, presided over by Archbishop Theodore, the British Church was condemned as non-Catholic.[27]

Wilfrid, at an assembly at Nesterfield, near Ripon, A.D. 705, declared, 'Was not I the first after the death of those great men sent by St. Gregory, to root out the poisonous seeds sown by Scottish missionaries? Was it not I who converted and brought the whole nation of the Northumbrians to the true Easter and Roman tonsure?'[28]

In A.D. 705 Adelm wrote to the Britons as being outside the 'Catholic' Church. 'The precepts of your bishops', he says, 'are not in accord with Catholic faith.[29] . . . We adjure you not to persevere in your arrogant contempt of the decrees of St. Peter and the traditions of the Roman Church by a proud and tyrannical attachment to the statutes of your ancestors.'[30]

The British Church, now openly declared heretical by Rome, struggled on for a time as a separate Church, and was known, particularly from this time, by the original title, 'The Culdee Church', as distinct from the Roman, and its ecclesiastics referred to by the Latin intruders as the 'British clergy'.

Adamnan, the first of the Ionian Culdees to swerve from the faith, strained every nerve to reduce the monks of Iona to Roman Catholic obedience. Bede says that Adamnan in A.D. 679 visited the churches of Northumbria and Ireland and brought almost all of them that were not under the domination of Hii (Iona) to the 'Catholic' unity.

The resistance of the premier monastery (Iona), the abbot of which was viewed as the primate of all the Hibernian bishops, prevailed for a time to retain their liberties. By the eleventh century, however, the Iona Church had become thoroughly Romanized, and had sunk into comparative unimportance.

Of Palladius, a Culdee of the fifth century who had visited Rome and had become a Romanizing bishop, Fordun says: 'Before whose coming the Scots had, as teachers of the faith and administers of the Sacraments, presbyters only and monks, following the order of the primitive Church.'[31]

Kentigern (St. Mungo), A.D. 514, is numbered among those who adorned the name of Culdee: for many years he was the disciple of St. Servan at Culross who taught and preached there as a Christian missionary, according to the system of the ancient British Church.

The Culdees or British clergy were, from Augustine's day, in constant collision with the Roman clergy; the Culdees seem to have been too much in love with simple Bible truth to find favour with those who aimed at wealth and power. Even the Venerable Bede could not escape the prejudices of his 'modern' times, saying: 'The Culdees followed uncertain rules in the observance of the great festival (Easter), practising only such works of piety and chastity as they could learn from the prophetical, evangelical and apostolical writings.'[32]

It is of consequence to note that in the early accounts which we have of the state of the Church, the final appeal in all doctrinal questions is to the Scriptures. It was remarked by Polydore Vergil that Gildas, in his long letter on the state of the Britons, quoted no book but the Bible,[33] and certainly his quotations from it show on the part of the British historian a very thorough acquaintance with the Word of God. At this period of the Church (fifth century) the Scriptures were very generally disseminated,[34] and men used such translations of the sacred text as commended themselves to their own judgment. The withholding of the Bible from the people and the exclusion of every translation from use but the Latin translation, even among the ministers of the Church, belonged to the ecclesiastical legislation of a later and more corrupt age; an age when ecclesiastical power came to be based not on the intelligence but on the ignorance of the people.[35]

The Culdee or British Church had pervaded Britain with the knowledge of the Gospel, and for centuries after the domination of Rome the Culdees continued to hold services frequently in the same Church with Roman priests.

The catalogues of their books show beyond a doubt that the ancient British ecclesiastics were not destitute of literary culture.[36]

Corruption was powerfully retarded by the firmness of the hierarchy of the Culdees; they were looked up to as the depositaries of the original national faith, and were most highly respected for sanctity and learning. They acquired great missionary zeal and great numbers of them went forth as missionaries and Christianized the whole of Europe from Iceland to the Danube.[37] This is a fact of history which has been diligently suppressed, but it is a fact which cannot be denied. It is remarkable that while the Church of Rome was sending her emissaries to "Christianize' the Saxons, the Celtic Church was sending her missionaries to convey the Gospel of salvation to France.[38]

Dr. Wylie says: 'It was the Culdee lamp that

burned at Constance, at Basle, at Ypres, at Worms
and Mainz. Boniface, the emissary of Rome, came
afterwards to put out these lights. The real apostle of
the provinces was the Culdee Church.'

A study of the history of the Culdee Church shows
that wherever the influence of Rome prevailed its
clergy were removed; not, however, without resistance.
But the struggle was a hopeless one. The Charter of
David of Scotland (1084–1155), who was an adherent
of the Latin Church, runs thus : 'David rex Scotorum,
etc. Be it known, that we have granted to the Canons
of St. Andrews the Island of Loch Leven, that they
may establish there a Canonical Order; and if the
Culdees who shall be found there, remain with them,
living according to rule, they may continue to do so
in peace; but if any one of them resist, we order
hereby that he be ejected from the island.'

In this high-handed manner was the property of
the Church transferred to the Roman hierarchy. Only
a century earlier Macbeth and his queen are recorded
in the register of this same Priory of St. Andrews as
the liberal benefactors of the Culdee monastery at
Loch Leven.[39]

The property which the Culdees held in their own
right was gradually confiscated by the Latin hierarchy
until the day came when they were dispossessed of
everything, including their ancient privileges, and were
absorbed into the Cathedral Chapters of the Roman
Church.[40]

Ledwich, the Irish antiquarian, says : 'The Culdees
did not adopt the corruptions and superstitions which
had contaminated Christianity for centuries. They

preserved their countrymen from the baleful contagion and, at length, fell a sacrifice in defence of the
ancient faith. Superstition found in them her most
determined foes. The Culdees continued until a new
race of monks arose, as inferior to them in learning
and piety as they surpassed them in wealth and
ceremonies, by which they captivated the eyes and
infatuated the hearts of men. The conduct of the
Romanizers towards the Culdees was uniformly
persecuting; and by force, cunning and seduction of
every kind, by degrees bereft them of their privileges
and institutions.'[41]

The monks of the papal Church were almost
wholly employed in metaphysical or chronological
disputes, legends, miracles and martyrologies—a sad
contrast to the pure Scriptural teaching disseminated
by the Culdees.

The history of the Culdee Church in Ireland is
largely the history of that Church in England,
Scotland and Wales, except that in the case of Ireland
she did not come, nationally, under the domination
of Rome until 1172, five centuries later than in
England. From this fact may be accounted the theory
held by many historians that the Culdee and Irish
Church were synonymous terms, and that from it the
Culdees spread to other parts of Britain and, further,
it accounts for the strength of that Church in Ireland
centuries after its submission to papal claims in
England and elsewhere.

O'Driscoll, a noted Roman Catholic writer, states:
'The ancient Order of the Culdees existed in Ireland
previous to Patrick; and all their institutions proved

that they were derived from a different origin from that of Rome.[42] This celebrated Order gave many eminent men to the Irish Church, and to Scotland and to other parts of the world, among whom Columbkill has still a name in Ireland as venerable and revered as that of Patrick himself. The Church discipline of the Culdees seems to have afforded the model for the modern Presbyterian establishment of Scotland.'[43]

The mission of Palladius in A.D. 421 signally failed. His effort to introduce papal Christianity in Wicklow met with firm resistance, and shortly afterwards he left the country.[44]

The following year, St. Patrick, who belonged to the Culdee Church, began his work as a missionary revivalist. Christianity, according to Gildas, had been introduced to Ireland three and a half centuries earlier and, according to tradition, about the same date by Caradoc, the Silurian king. Caradoc, it is said, while a prisoner at Rome, was converted to Christianity by St. Paul, and it is to his children, Linus and Claudia, and his son-in-law Pudens, that St. Paul sends greetings in his second letter to Timothy.

From the days of St. Patrick to the reign of Henry II the Church in Ireland was renowned, not only for its learning but for its missionary zeal. Its evangelists spread the light of Truth wherever they travelled in Britain and to many places on the Continent, where the monasteries (afterwards Romanized) were set up on Culdee foundations. To these, many of the Culdee monks fled for refuge in the ninth and tenth centuries when Ireland was so sorely ravaged by the Danes. They took with them, for safety, many of their precious manuscripts, which may, in a future day, should they be discovered, throw valuable light on the early Christian Church in these Islands.

O'Driscoll presents a true picture of the early Irish Church when he says: 'The Christian Church of that country, as founded by St. Patrick, existed for many centuries free and unshackled. For about seven hundred years this Church maintained its independence. It had no connection with England, and differed on points of importance from Rome. The first work of Henry II was to reduce the Church of Ireland into obedience to the Roman Pontiff. Accordingly he procured a Council of Irish Clergy to be held in Cashel in 1172, and the combined influence and intrigues of Henry and the Pope prevailed. This Council put an end to the ancient Church of Ireland; she submitted to the yoke of Rome. This ominous apostasy has been followed by a series of calamities hardly to be equalled in the world. From the days of Patrick to the Council of Cashel was a bright and glorious career for Ireland. From the sitting of the Council to our own times the lot of Ireland has been unmixed evil and all her history a tale of woe.'[45]

The following letter tells a curious story. It is from the Bishop of Mentz to Shane O'Neill, the Irish chief and rebel, dated from Rome, April 28th, 1528, in the name of the Pope and Cardinals: 'My dear Son O'Neill—Thou and thy fathers are all along faithful to the Mother Church of Rome. His Holiness Paul III, now Pope, and the Council of the Holy Fathers there, have lately found a prophecy of one St. Lazerianus, an Irish Bishop of Cashel, wherein he saith that the Mother Church of Rome falleth, when in Ireland the Catholic faith is overcome. Therefore, for the glory of the Mother Church, the honour of St. Peter, and your own secureness, suppress heresy and His Holiness's enemies, for when the Roman faith there perisheth, the See of Rome falleth also. Therefore, the Council of Cardinals have thought fit to encourage your Country of Ireland as a Sacred Island; being certified, whilst the Mother Church hath a son of worth as yourself, and those that shall succour you and join therein, that she will never fall, but have more or less hold in Britain, in spite of fate.'[46] This letter was written in the reign of Henry VIII when the first indications were received with alarm by the Roman hierarchy, of the approaching end of papal domination and of the mighty change about to take place in these realms.

[1] Oxford Icelandic Dictionary.
[2] See Prelim. Dissert. Laing's *Heimskrongla*, p. 86.
[3] See H. Munro Chadwick, *The Origin of the English*, p. 321.
[4] Oxford Icelandic Dictionary.
[5] Rollaston, *Mazzaroth*, III, 23.
[6] Bruce Hannay, *European and Other Race Origins*, p. 456.
[7] *Annals of England*, Vol. I, p. 164.
[8] Geoffrey of Monmouth, Bk. XI, Chap. X.
[9] Palgrave, *History of the Anglo-Saxons*, p. 44.
[10] Geoffrey of Monmouth, Bk. XI, Chap. XII.
[11] Brit. MSS. quoted in the second volume of the Horae Britannicae, p. 267. Spelman's *Concilia*, p. 108.
[12] Bede, E. H., Chap. II, 2. Haddan & Stubbs, *Councils,* III, 38. *Hist. of Wales* (1911), p. 173.
[13] Bacon, *Government of England*, p. 13.
[14] *Laws of England*, Vol. IV, p. 105.
[15] Hengwst MSS. Geoffrey of Monmouth, Bk. XI, Chap. XII. Humphrey Lloyd, *Sebright MSS.*

[16] Caerwys, MSS.

[17] Paton, *Brit. History and Papal Claims*, p. 4.

[18] Bede, *Eccles. History*, Bk. III, Chap. 4.

[19] Paper in the *Ecclesiastic* for April 1864 on Dr. Todd's *St. Patrick*. Concilia Constantiano Theodore-Martin (Lovar), 1517.

[20] McCallum, *History of the Culdees*, pp. 60, 61.

[21] Ban-gor, *Magnus Circulus*.

[22] MS. in the Mostyn Collection.

[23] *Annals Cambraiae*, CLVII.

[24] D'Aubigne, *History Reform*, Vol. V. Milman, *History of Latin Christianity*, Vol. II, p. 234. *Annales Cambraiae*, VLXIX.

[25] Malmes, *History of the Kings*, p. 308.

[25] Malmes., *History of the Kings*, p. 308.

[27] Haddon & Stubbs, III, pp. 256 ff.

[28] Montalembert, *Monks of the West*, Vol. IV, p. 79.

[29] Adelmi opp., ed. Giles, pp. 24 ff. Monumenta Germ. History Tom, III, pp. 231 ff.

[30] *Monks of the West*, Vol. IV, p. 233.

[31] Scotichron, Lib. III, Chap. VIII.

[32] *Eccles. History*, III, Chap. IV.

[33] *De Excid. Britt.*

[34] Williams, *Early Christianity in Britain*, p. 447. Ulphilos, Bishop of the Goths (A.D. 38), MS. in the Library of Upsal Naseau, VIII, 40.

[35] *Vide* Ussher's *Historia Dogmatica*.

[36] Keith Bish. App., p. 5871. *Regist Priorat*, St. Andree, p. 17.

[37] Dasent, Introduction to *Burnt-Nyal*, p. vii. *De Mensura Orbis*, written by Dicuil an Irish monk, in the year A.D. 835.

[38] D'Aubigne, *Hist. of the Reformation*, Vol. IV. McLauchlan *The Early Scottish Church*, p. 216: 'There was a Continental mission scheme in Scotland as early at 588.'

[39] Registrum Prioralus St. Andree, p. 188, Keith Catalogue of Scottish Bishops, p. 9.

[40] Alexander, *Ter-Centenary of the Scottish Reformation* (Edin. 1860), pp. 13, 17.

[41] Ledwich's *Antiquities*.

[42] *Vide* Reeve's *Culdees*, p. 25.

[43] *Hist. of Ireland*, pp. 26, 27.

[44] Bury, *Life of St. Patrick*, pp. 44, 45.

[45] *Views of Ireland*, Vol. II, p. 84.

[46] Mant's, *History of the Irish Church*, p. 140.

CHAPTER XII

CULDEE INFLUENCE

CONQUERERS are not usually disposed to speak with much kindness or respect of those whom they have overcome or dispossessed. It was so between the successful priests of the Roman hierarchy and the ecclesiastics of the ancient Church of the Culdees, whom they had succeeded in supplanting. But it is significant that the British continued, in after times, to cherish the highest esteem for the memory of these men of piety and power who had distinguished their ancient national church. Rome might have supplanted the Culdee Church; she could not eradicate from the minds of the people the principles it had imparted.

It requires but little acquaintance with British history to observe that these principles never were eradicated, and that during the reign of the Roman Church in these islands they continued to exist. Men like Alcuin in his Caroline books; John Scotus, the protégé of King Alfred; and Archbishop Elfric with his 'Saxon Homily', endeavoured to stem the tide of doctrinal error.

King Alfred, a great patron of literature, gave to his people, in the ninth century, the Gospels in the Saxon tongue—a life work worthy of record. We find from a letter of King Alfred's that he wrote: 'I wish you to know that it often occurs to my mind to consider what manner of wise men there were formerly in the British nation, both spiritual and temporal; I considered how earnest God's ministers then were about preaching as about learning in this land.'[1]

The following is an extract from a sermon of Bonar's : 'In some of the islands which we are apt to consider as the seat of ignorance and barbarism, lived a people remarkable for simplicity of manners, purity of behaviour and unaffected piety (Culdees). Of their number were Columba and his brethren. Even in the tenth century when the darkness of corruption and error had greatly increased we are told there were some godly men in Scotland who taught the true doctrine of Christ's atonement and continued to receive their functions apart without acknowledging the authority of those who assumed authority over God's inheritance.'

The Rev. C. G. Meissner writes : 'At the time of the Synod of Whitby the Christianity of Mercia was entirely Celtic in character, no Roman missionary had ever penetrated to the kingdom. . . . The Synod of Whitby left the position of the monastery of Lindisfarne absolutely unchanged, and not until 1138 did the last of those Celtic customs which had held their ground so tenaciously in the Church of Lindisfarne, come to an end.'[2] And Dr. Barry affirms: 'Monks whose home was Iona or Lindisfarne helped to make England Christian from the Cheviots to the Thames. But Augustine, Paulinus and Wilfrid of York made it Roman in hierarchy, ritual and learning.'[3]

One of the papal entreaties by which Henry II was induced to conquer Ireland related to the possibility of bringing the Christian Church of Ireland into conformity with Rome.

Archbishop Lanfranc of Canterbury was horrified at hearing that they did not pray to saints, dedicate churches to the Virgin Mary, nor use the Roman service, and even St. Bernard in his distant retreat was greatly distressed when he heard of the Irish Culdees. In his righteous wrath he stigmatized them as 'Absolute barbarians, a stubborn, stiff-necked and ungovernable generation and abominable; Christian in name but in reality *pagan*.'

The Culdees upheld the institution of marriage among the clergy and their abbacies were frequently hereditary. Archbishop Ussher asserted that the Northern Irish 'continued in their old tradition in spite of various papal bulls'.

It is on record that Culdees officiated in the Church of St. Peter, York, up to A.D. 936,[4] and according to Raine, the Canons of York were called Culdees as late as the reign of Henry II.

In the Cotton collection in the British Museum is preserved a privilege which King Ethelred is said to have granted to the Church of Canterbury in A.D. 1016. Dr. Lingard, who first drew attention to the terms of the privilege, observes that in the charters the prebendaries are termed 'Cultores Clerici', which seems to indicate that the collegiate clergy were even then styled Culdees in the South as well as in the North of England.[5]

In the tenth century the Pictish king, Constantine

II, according to the Register of St. Andrews, 'having resigned the kingdom according to God's will became Abbot of the Culdees at St. Andrews'.[6]

The Culdees of St. Andrews continued long to form the Chapter of the Cathedral, and claimed the right of electing the bishop.[7]

From the same Register of St. Andrews we learn: 'The Culdees continued to perform Divine worship in a certain corner of the Church after their own manner, nor could this evil be removed till the time of King Alexander in 1124 so that the Culdees and popish priests performed their services in the same Church for nearly three hundred years.'

The Culdees had in Abernethy a university and a collegiate church which is known to have subsisted toward the end of the thirteenth century and they were observed in Kyle and Cunningham until the followers of Wycliffe appeared, like the faint daybreak of the Reformation.[8]

Ledwich states that at Mondincha in Tipperary as late as 1185 a Culdean abbey and church still stood 'whose clergy had not conformed to the reigning superstition, but devoutly served God in this wild and dreary retreat, sacrificing all the flattering prospects of the world for their ancient doctrine and discipline'.[9]

Giraldus Cambrensis, who went to Ireland with King John, mentions the same abbey: 'In North Munster is a lake containing two isles, in the lesser is a chapel where a few monks called Culdees devoutly serve God.'[10]

Archbishop Ussher (1581–1656) says of these ecclesiastics of the ancient British Church: 'In the greater churches of Ulster, as at Cluanimnis (Clones) and Daminni (Devenish) and at Armagh in our own memory there were priests called Culdees who celebrated Divine Service in the Choir. Their president was styled Prior of the Culdees and acted as precentor.'[11]

One, Cornelius Sheridan, the Culdee sacristan of Devenish, *circa* 1428, and Pierce O'Flanagan, prior and sacristan of Culdees, are names that have come down to us as 'defenders of the Faith'.[12]

In Ireland the ancient title survived the Reformation and existed in the year 1628 when a deed was executed in which the lessor was 'Edward Burton, prior of the Cathedral Church of Armagh, on behalf of the vicars Choral and Culdees of the same'.[13] Bishop Worth, in his rental of Killaloe drawn up in 1667, adds, as a note to the thirty-three canons, 'These in Ulster are called Culdees.'[14]

It has been said that were we to search for that which most resembles the Culdee Church in modern times, we would find it in those great educational and missionary establishments which the Scottish Churches have planted in India, where a body of earnest, enlightened men are engaged in teaching and preaching the Gospel, paying occasional visits to outlying towns and villages and having occasional interviews with princes, for the purpose of communicating the knowledge of saving Truth.[15]

With all their imperfections the Protestant Churches of Britain are the representatives of the original Christian or Culdee Church founded in these islands in apostolic times. Even in the 'Dark Ages' Britain was never under the papacy to the extent that the Continental nations were.

If it were desired to strengthen, from the Roman Catholic documentary sources, the apostolical elements in the foundation of the British Church, or to insist that it can with equal justice, at least, claim, with the Roman Church, St. Peter amongst its founders, it would not be difficult to adduce the affirmative evidence of Roman Catholic authorities upon the point.[16] Cornelius à Lapide, in answering the question, 'How came St. Paul not to salute St. Peter in his Epistle to the Romans?', states, 'Peter, banished with the rest of the Jews from Rome by the edict of Claudius, was absent in Britain';[17] and Eusebius Pamphilius, A.D. 306, quoted by Simon Metaphrastes, considers Peter to have been in Britain as well as in Rome.[18]

The discovery at Whithorn of the stone known as the 'Peter Stone' seems to afford some support to the statements of these early writers. It is a rude pillar, some four feet high and fifteen inches wide. An inscription in debased Roman capitals reads: 'LOE (VS) S (ANC) TI PETRI APVSTOLI'—'The place of St. Peter the Apostle.' St. Peter would be, therefore, to the people of Britain a Culdich or 'refugee' from Rome in the reign of Claudius, A.D. 41–54, arriving in Britain a few years after the arrival of the 'Judean refugees' or Culdich (certain strangers) from Palestine in the last year of Tiberius, A.D. 37.

The vision to which St. Peter refers (2 *Peter* 1 : 14), 'Knowing that shortly I must put off this my tabernacle, even as the Lord Jesus Christ hath shewed me', is said to have appeared to him in Britain on the spot where once stood the British Church of Lambedr (St. Peter) and now stands the Abbey of St. Peter, Westminster.[19]

In considering evidence in support of the belief that St. Paul visited Britain it is of consequence to note that the tradition that he did so has been accepted by numerous writers, including Ussher and Stillingfleet.[20]

In the fourth century Theodoret wrote, 'St. Paul brought salvation to the isles in the ocean',[21] and also mentions the Britons among the converts of the Apostles, and in the same century Jerome states that St. Paul's evangelical labours extended to the western parts. In the sixth century Venantius, and in the seventh the Patriarch of Jerusalem, speak expressly of St. Paul's mission to Britain.[22]

After the Synod of Whitby the whole organization of the British Church was gradually remodelled so that it would be exceedingly difficult to recognize the old Church of the first five centuries in the great hierarchial establishments of the Church of Rome. In the course of time, instead of the unpretentious Culdee establishment, there arose a powerful hierarchy, the members of which came to hold the highest offices in Church and State. This change in the Church, accompanied with the accumulation of wealth by rich endowments, and the high offices (often filled by foreigners) was repugnant to the native population who had long bravely defended their country, and filled the offices in Church and State well, and who were now put aside, their liberties withheld and their property confiscated.

Continual friction and frequent outbursts of resistance to its encroachments marked the whole period of Rome's attempted domination in Britain and are exhibited in such outbreaks as the letter of King Robert Bruce and his nobles to Pope John, the uprising of the Lollards, and finally the events of the Reformation. British independence, civil and ecclesiastical, is well expressed in the words of Robert Bruce: 'It is not Glory; it is not Riches; neither is it Honour; but it is Liberty alone that we fight and contend for, which no honest man will lose but with his life.'[23]

Edgar the Pacific, A.D. 959–975, fearlessly proclaimed in the presence of Dunstan (the first of the great ecclesiastical statesmen of whom Wolsey was the last) and with the enthusiastic approval of his nobles and the nation, as claiming no novelty but their immemorial right and liberty, that 'the King of England held the sword of Constantine, that he was in his own dominions the Lord's husbandman, the Pastor of pastors and the representative of Christ on earth'.[24]

The Roman hierarchy, it is now evident, actuated by such zeal against the Culdees, has not allowed them common historical justice. Their influence, however, remained, and these early protesters against a Romanized Church in these islands lived and worked, through evil report and good report, until the time in which the followers of Wycliffe appeared.

The love of the Scriptures to which the Culdees had trained the people, never entirely died out. To the early British or Culdee Church our country owes its Protestantism; its determination to exercise individual

freedom in religion; its love of the Scriptures and its
missionary zeal.

> 'The pure Culdees
> Were Albyn's earliest priests of God,
> Ere yet an island of her seas
> By foot of Saxon monk was trod.'
>
> Campbell 'Reullura'

[1] Alfred Praef. ad past., 85 Necephorus II, 40.

[2] *Celtic Church*, pp. 134, 158.

[3] *Papal Monarchy*, p. 58.

[4] Dugdale, *Monasticon Anglicanum*, Vol. V, II, p. 607.

[5] *History and Ant. of the Anglo-Saxon Church*, Vol. II,
Chap. XIII, p. 294 (ed. 1845).

[6] Innes, *Critical Essay*, Tom. II, p. 786.

[7] *Regist. Priorat St. Andree*, p. 49.

[8] Edin. Encyc., Vol. I.

[9] *Irish Antiquities*, pp. 102, 120.

[10] Topograph Hibern, Dist. II, Cap. IV (Camden's *Anglica*,
p. 716).

[11] *Britain Eccles. Antiq.*, Cap XV (Works Vol. VI, p. 174).

[12] Rev. Canon McKenna, M.R.I.A., 'Devenish', p. 93 of *Celtic
Church in Ireland*.

[13] Original in the Primate's Record Room, Armagh.

[14] Cotton's *Fasti Eccles. Hibern*, Vol. V, p. 66.

[15] McLaughlan, *The Early Scottish Church*, p. 164.

[16] See R. W. Morgan, *St. Paul in Britain*.

[17] Cornelius à Lapide, in *Argum epist. St. Pauli ad Romanos*,
Chap. XVI.

[18] Metaphrastes ad 29 Junii. Menalogii Graeceorum.

[19] Dean Stanley, *Mem. of Westminster Abbey*, Chap. I, p. 18.

[20] See Rev. W. Hughes, *Church of the Cymry*, p. 15.

[21] *Intepr. in Psalm 116*, opp. Lut. Par. 1642.

[22] Ussher, *Brit. Eccles. Antiq.*, p. 4.

[23] T. Wright, *History of Scotland*, Vol. I, p. III.

[24] Twysden, *Scriptores*, X, p. 360.

CHAPTER XIII

THE REFORMATION

A COMMON knowledge of history and a very little research would suffice to prove that the work of the Culdees, who became, from the first encroachment of Rome, the British protestors, never quite died out, and that the Reformation in these islands began long anterior to the date usually assigned to it. It was the struggle for religious rights which opened men's eyes to all their rights. It was resistance to religious usurpation which led men to withstand political oppression.

The first notable resistance to the Papacy as a step towards the Reformation was made by William the Conqueror. When Pope Gregory VII demanded homage of the king for his realm of England, William replied: 'Fealty I have never willed to do nor will I do it now. I have never promised, nor do I find that my predecessors did it to yours.'[1]

William never permitted his clergy to be governed by the will of the Pope and when Lanfranc, Archbishop of Canterbury, was summoned by that dignitary to appear before him at Rome to answer for the rebellious conduct of the English king, William refused to let him proceed.[2]

William never bowed before the papacy, yet we must not make the mistake of thinking him a Protestant as we now understand the term. While he overcame all papal attempts to gain political ascendancy in England the spiritual power of the Latin Church remained for centuries the dominant, though waning, power in this country.

Along with the fact that the Culdees existed down to the days of Wycliffe should be placed the statement that it was said in his day, 'You could not meet two men on the road but one was a Wycliffite.' The Reformation, which was commenced in England by Wycliffe, was 136 years earlier than Luther, and probably half the nation followed him.

While Wycliffe was translating the Scriptures, and preparing the way for Reformation principles, another reformer in the person of Edward III was taking the first steps towards the sweeping away of papal jurisdiction from the national Church.

Edward III, following in the footsteps of the British king, Arthur, the founder of the 'Round Table', whom he appears to have made his ideal, identified himself all through his reign with the interests of the national Church against the encroaching claims of the Roman See.[3] The threat of the Pope to cite him to appear at his Court of Avignon to answer for his defaults in not performing the homage nor paying the tribute to the See of Rome, undertaken and guaranteed by John, King of England, for himself and his heirs, was submitted by Edward to Parliament for their advice; it was given by the Bishops, Lords and Commons after full deliberation in the following memorable words: 'That neither King John nor any other king could bring himself, his realm and people under such subjection without their assent . . . that if done it was without the consent of Parliament and contrary to his coronation oath, and that in case the Pope should attempt to constrain the king and his subjects to perform what he lays claim to, they would resist and withstand him to the uttermost of their power.'[1]

Instructing his chaplain, William of Wykeham, who was also his surveyor and secretary, to make inquiries into the tradition of the Order of St. George and the Garter, it was revealed that the British Church of the first five centuries had been entirely free from papal control and that one of the first acts of Arthur's reign had been to refuse the tribute demanded by special emissaries sent from Rome. It may have been this precedent, set by his predecessor, that determined King Edward to obtain a Bull from Pope Clement VI (1348) declaring the Chapel of St. George a free Chapel, free that is, as had been the early British Church, from papal jurisdiction.

The Sovereign—the head of the Order—and the Bishop of Winchester, the Prelate, nominated the Deans and Canons of the Chapel, with appeal to the visitor, the Lord Chancellor. The Royal Chapel of St. George, Windsor, may therefore claim to be the foundation-stone of the Reformation, and a religious foundation, thoroughly organized in every detail of its constitution by fifty-four original statutes. St. George's College is the first in England founded 'free' of the control of abbot or prior and its statutes have been the model upon which all post-Reformation and collegiate staffs have been moulded.

The Marquis of Lorne, a former Constable of Windsor Castle, reminds us that Windsor takes precedence of Westminster Abbey, and that the succession of Deans and Canons has not been interrupted for six centuries.[5]

Edward III may be said to have forged another link in the chain of resistance to Rome's claim to supremacy which culminated in the final secession under Henry VIII two hundred years later.

The revival of the Arthurian traditions by Edward III along with the establishment of the British Order of the Goodly Fellowship of Chivalry had, as its founder, King Arthur, the first of the Knights. It is recorded how 'Edward, king of England, at this time resolved to rebuild the great castle of Windsor formerly built and founded by King Arthur; and where first was set up and established the noble Round Table from which so many men have issued forth to perform feats of arms and prowess throughout the world'.[6]

King Arthur, it is said, modelled his Round Table Fellowship on the Table of the Last Supper. As a descendant of Joseph of Arimathea, who led a company of persecuted Christians—Judean refugees, or Culdees—to our shores, the details of those early days would be, to Arthur, family history, for most, if not all of his knights, were of the family of Joseph.[7] The Round Table, which now hangs on the wall of Winchester Great Hall, is a reminder to the nation of the sacred nature of the foundation upon which the 'Round Table Fellowship' rests. Henry VIII, on the occasion of the visit of Charles V, had the table taken down and re-painted green and white, the liveries of the British Order and the rose of St. George in the centre. The names of the Companions of the Goodly Fellowship inscribed on the margin by the Tudor monarch have been identified, with but one exception, as owners of castles and estates in Monmouthshire, South Wales and Cornwall. We have thus, through Arthurian history, a link with the early British or Culdee Church and a very definite link with Palestine, a link which no other country holds in its historical records.

The Duke of Lancaster, known to history as 'John of Gaunt', son of Edward III, feudal to the core, resented the official arrogance of the prelates and the large share which they drew to themselves of the temporal power, and made alliance with Wycliffe, who dreamed of restoring by apostolic poverty its long-lost apostolic purity to the clergy. From points so opposite and with aims so contradictory, were they united to reduce the wealth and humble the pride of the Roman hierarchy.

Another factor which gave a tremendous impetus to the work of purification from the errors of Rome was the number of economic difficulties in the days of Wycliffe, caused by the 'Black Death', which prepared the hearts of the people to receive a reformed Christian religion.

Dean Milman, a nineteenth-century scholar, states with regard to *Piers the Ploughman*, written about this time, A.D. 1362, by William Langlande, 'The people who could listen with delight to such strains were far advanced towards a revolt from Latin Christianity. Truth, true religion, was not to be found with, it was not known by, Pope, Cardinals, Bishops,

Clergy, Monks or Friars. It was to be found by man himself, by the individual man, by the poorest man, under the sole guidance of reason and the Grace of God, vouchsafed directly, not through any intermediate human being, or even sacrament, to the self-directing soul. There is a manifest appeal throughout, an unconscious installation of Scripture alone, as the final judge.'[8]

A faithful protestor, Archbishop Aelfric's work aptly fulfilled his Hebrew name 'God our Redeemer'. The profound piety of his Paschal Homily (about A.D. 1000) and its insistence on the spiritual as opposed to the carnal presence of Christ in the Lord's Supper were truly worthy of 'an Israelite indeed'.

The petty revenge of Rome in taking up the remains of Wycliffe in 1428, forty-four years after his death, and casting them into the waters of the Swift, served only to add a new lustre to the fame of the Reformer. As the historian Thomas Fuller says: 'The little river conveyed Wycliffe's remains into the Avon, the Avon into the Severn, the Severn into the narrow seas, and they into the main ocean. And thus the ashes of Wycliffe are the emblem of his doctrine which now are dispersed all over the world.'[9]

Huss had received the light from Wycliffe and he, with his co-workers Jerome, Latimer and Ridley, and Wycliffe's followers, the Lollards, were links in the chain between Wycliffe and the Reformation.

The protest against the supremacy of the Pope in this land, based upon the laws of the kingdom, was another cause which impelled Britain towards the day of Reformation. The glorious day of greater light and liberty was, however, far off. Ignorance was widespread, and its saddest phase was the decay of the knowledge of the word of God. The Bible was locked up from the people because it was written in Hebrew, Greek or the Latin into which Jerome had translated the Scriptures. The unlearned people had no power whereby to open the Divine treasure-house until they were given the Bible in the English language.

The clergy also, with the laity, appear to have been in great ignorance concerning the Scriptures. Rome well knew that reading the Bible intelligently stimulates inquiry, extends the realm of thought and emancipates the mind from slavery to mere human authority.

In the time of Pope Alexander VI (1492), so ignorant were some of the clergy that a French monk said: 'They have now found out a new language called Greek; we must carefully guard ourselves against it. That language will be the mother of all sorts of heresies. I see in the hands of a great number of persons a book written in this language called "The New Testament"; it is a book full of brambles, with vipers in them. As to the Hebrew, whoever learns that becomes a Jew at once.'[10]

We read in Luther's 'Table Talk' of an Archbishop of Mainz coming across a copy of the Bible, and on examining it was quite puzzled as to what it could be. When he began to read it he was so taken aback that he exclaimed: 'Of a truth I do not know what book this is, but I perceive everything in it is against us.'

With the invention of printing in the late fourteenth century, the preachings and writings of the Reformers were gradually spread among the people, not, however, without raising the opposition of the Roman hierarchy. The Vicar of Croydon, preaching at St. Paul's Cross in the days of Henry VIII, declared that either the Roman Church must abolish printing or printing would abolish her!

Caxton's press was established in the almonry at Westminster, a little enclosure containing a chapel and alms-houses. A red pole showed the seeker where the printed books could be bought 'good chepe'. Not the people only but kings favoured the wonderful new process. Rome alone discouraged it. At her General Council in 1514, held at Mantua by command of Pope Paul the Third, to which the King of England among other princes refused either to come or send at the Pope's call, Rome forbade the printing of any books without her permission.[11]

About this time several translations of the Scriptures were printed and circulated. Miles Coverdale assisted Tyndale in re-translating the Pentateuch about 1530, and shortly afterwards, in 1535, appeared his own translation of the Bible. Two years later another translation appeared — that of John Rogers the Martyr, and in 1539 the translation of Taverner, another Cambridge man. Rogers was the first to be brought to the stake in the five dark years of Mary's reign.

The Reformation of the Church was further manifested in the Revised Prayer Book promulgated by the Act of 1559, and by the 39 Articles of 1563. We cannot doubt that, in answer to many prayers, the

Holy Spirit guided the minds of the bishops and pastors of Christ's flock in these national confessions of faith, as well as in the publication of the Bishop's Bible in 1568 and later the Authorized Version.[12]

One of the most interesting events of Edward VI's short reign was the publication of the second Prayer Book. Many of the imperfections of the first Prayer Book were removed, and the result, with some further revision in Elizabeth's reign, is the 'Book of Common Prayer' used today in the English Church services.

With the passing of Mary of England, and the accession of Queen Elizabeth, came the feeling throughout the land that brighter days had dawned; imprisoned Protestant witnesses for the Faith were freed with the joyful assurance that the reign of the stake was over.

The long reign of Queen Elizabeth was noted for the overthrow of every concession to the papacy. Elizabeth sincerely resolved to restore Protestantism, but the work was attended with serious dangers. Most of the clergy were papists, for the notable and learned divines and Gospel preachers had passed away in fiery martyrdom.

Yet in spite of all difficulties Elizabeth kept on her course without flinching. One of her first acts was to forbid the elevation of the Host at the Mass, to enjoin that the Litany, Epistle and the Gospel be read in English, and that all preaching be forbidden except by those who had obtained special licence. The necessity for this step was that as the majority of the clergy were papists, sermons against the Reformed doctrines would have been preached had they been permitted.

It is true that Missa, or Mass (Feast), was an early name for the Lord's Supper. Eucharist (Thanksgiving) was earlier, and Liturgy (Public Service) earlier still, but it should be remembered that the celebration of Mass must then have been actually very different from what it became, and was, at the time of the Reformation. In the Church of Rome it became inter-woven with extraordinary ceremony and erroneous ritual. 'High Mass' was the choral version sung in Latin when the Host (the elements) were lifted to be worshipped. The original simple beauty of the Communion Service was lost—the priests only were allowed the privilege of partaking of the bread and wine, the laity sometimes individually on a death-bed. The Reformed Church of England restored the Communion Service to the people as in the primitive Church. To reclaim this was the Reformer's hardest battle, but they won. In the very early days of the Reformation the Mass service remained as well as the Holy Communion service, at which the laity partook —but finally 'Mass' was abolished. In the primitive Church nothing but a general communion (sharing together) was ever contemplated, as seen by Justin Martyr's description, A.D. 140.[13]

When the Archbishop of York, Nicholas Heath, who refused to take the oath of supremacy, exhorted Elizabeth to follow the Pope, she gave him a memorable reply : 'I will answer you in the words of Joshua. As Joshua said of himself and his, "I and my realm will serve the Lord." My sister [Mary] could not bind

the realm, nor bind those who should come after her,
to submit to a usurped authority. I take those who
maintain here the Bishop of Rome and his ambitious
pretensions, to be enemies to God and to me.'[14]

The Elizabethan 'Act of Uniformity' enjoined all
ministers 'to say, and use, the Matins, Evensong,
Celebration of the Lord's Supper, etc., as authorized
by Parliament in the fifth and sixth year of Edward
VI.' This Act, aimed only against papists, became
afterwards a bitter yoke to many Protestants.

A large Bible, a Book of Homilies, and Erasmus's
'Paraphrase of the New Testament', were ordered to
be placed in every church at the expense of the parish;
while Sunday after Sunday the reading of the Scriptures in English, and the Homilies, was gradually
enlightening those who sat in darkness.

The progress of the Reformation received every
encouragement from those exiles who had taken
refuge in Zurich, Geneva and Strasbourg, but had
now returned to England when they heard that the
black night had passed away. Among these must be
mentioned Bishop Jewel, the author of the famous
work entitled *The Apology of the Church of England*.
It was written in Latin because it was addressed to
all Europe as the answer of the Reformed National
Church of England to those Roman Catholics who
said that the Reformation had set up a new Church.
Jewel rightly contended that the Reformers were
returning to the primitive Church of the first century
as founded by the Apostles, and this was not in any
way a novel Church.[15]

As in England, so in Ireland, the yoke of Rome

was cast aside by the national Church at the Reformation. The Very Rev. R. G. S. King, M.A., Dean of Derry, in his brochure on St. Patrick, states: 'When Elizabeth was carrying out the Reformation, ten of the Irish bishops had been bishops under Henry VIII. If you had told them they belonged to a new Church they simply would not have understood you. Removal of abuses nor changes in a Prayer Book do not make a new Church. . . . The simple historical truth is, there was no break in the continuity of the Church of Ireland at the Reformation, and every attempt to prove the contrary has only resulted in confirmation of its unbroken descent from the ancient Church of our native land.' Thus the Reformation was established, though not perfected, in the days of Elizabeth, and the yoke of Rome, imposed unwittingly by King Oswy in A.D. 664, thrown aside nine centuries later by Queen Elizabeth; the cleansing of the sanctuary had begun.

On one occasion, in a speech before Parliament, Queen Elizabeth declared: 'This much I must say, that some faults and negligences may grow and be in the Church, whose overruler God hath made me. . . . All which, if you, my Lords of the Clergy do not amend, I mean to depose you. Look you, therefore, well to your charges.'[16]

It was a determined policy of Queen Elizabeth to put a stop to papal intrusion upon her authority in her realm, and in the pursuit of this policy many papists suffered death for political offences. Religious persecution, however, occupied no place in Elizabeth's policy, and it was her joyful boast that no Romanist had been put to death during her reign on account of his religion. Whatever may be said to lessen the contrast favourable to her reign in this respect, in comparison with the previous reign, it is sufficiently marked to be thoroughly appreciated by all but the prejudiced.

The character of the early British Church was now in a great measure restored. It must not be forgotten, however, that the Church at no time was without its protesters, the Culdees, worshipping God according to the practice of the primitive Church in these islands, and frequently in the same Church with Latin priests. As related in the previous chapter, the Culdees were known to have existed down to the seventeenth century. The Acts of Parliament and Convocations continuously made it clear that the Church and the nation once for all took their stand before God and man on the immutable rock of Holy Scripture, to proclaim 'the everlasting gospel' and rule the people by His laws; thrusting aside papal pretensions as an impertinence and usurpation.

From the Reformation onward the Protestant Church did not maintain that intense zeal which her earlier supporters displayed; apathy crept in, and divisions and sub-divisions occurred, weakening her cause throughout the land.

As early as 1689 a desire for unity in Protestantism was expressed by Archbishop Sancroft in an admonition to his clergy, and in his own very tender regard to our brethren, the 'Protestant Dissenters'. He exhorts his clergy to 'take all opportunities of assuring these non-conforming brethren that the Bishops of this

Church are really and sincerely irreconcilable enemies to the errors of the Church of Rome, and that the very unkind jealousies which some have had of us to the contrary were altogether groundless. And, in the last place, that they warmly and most affectionately exhort them to join with us in daily fervent prayer to the God of peace, for the universal blessed union of all Reformed Churches both at home and abroad against our common enemies, that all they who do confess the holy name of our dear Lord, and do agree in the truth of His Holy Word, may also meet in one Holy Communion, and live in perfect unity and godly love.'[17]

It has been said that the Episcopalian, the Presbyterian and the Independent can each discover in the early British Church the prototype of the system to which he adheres. Paton supports this view when he says: 'If the question be asked, was the organization of the Celtic Church in Scotland Episcopalian or Presbyterian, the answer of an impartial judge must be that it was neither the one nor the other, but an order, *sui generis*—a system of church policy which might develop into either, or even into something different from both.' It has also been said that the Elizabethan Church might, in the seventeenth century, have retained the Puritans if it had been wisely led. The saintship of the laity is the secret of the Puritan faith, and it is something which is vital to British Christianity.

Each denomination of Protestantism had behind it, at least, this common principle, the intention to be true to the purpose of our Lord as it was unfolded in the Apostolic writings.

There is much in the past history of the British nation for the thoughtful Protestant to study. The truth, however, does not lie on the surface. On the confession of Roman Catholic historians themselves our histories, both civil and ecclesiastical, have been written with an astonishing indifference to truth.

Dr. Barry, a historian of the Latin Church, declared : 'To manipulate ancient writings, to edit history in one's own favour, did not appear criminal —in the ages of faith—if the end in view were otherwise just and good'[18]; and Cardinal Newman, to whom a proposal had been made to found a Roman Catholic Review, replied : 'Who could bear it, unless one doctored all one's facts one would be thought a bad Catholic.'[19]

The undisputed writings of the early Christians began about seventy years after the time of the Apostles. At that period there probably remained none of the first converts or contemporaries of the Apostles. But there were living not a few who had been acquainted with the last survivors of that generation. When the Apostles died they must have left behind them a multitude who had known them. And of these not a few must have continued many years, and must have had association with the new generation which sprang up after the Apostolic age. In the time of that generation the series of Christian authors began, and they testify to the establishment of a Christian Church in Britain. The story of this Church is the story of the Light that never went out.

Cardinal Pole, in Queen Mary Tudor's reign, when reconciling England to the Pope and the Church of Rome, on two occasions deliberately and publicly said : 'England was the first country to receive Christianity.' Before Philip and Mary, seated under a canopy of state before the assembled Lords and Commons in the great chamber of Whitehall, he said : 'The Apostolic See from which I come, hath a special respect to this realm above all others, and not without cause, seeing that God Himself as it were by Providence hath given to this realm prerogative of nobility above all others, which to make plain unto you, that this island (first of all islands) received the light of Christian religion' (Fox's *Acts and Monuments,* Vol. VI, p. 568). The next day in Westminster Abbey before Philip and Mary in state and the Lord and Commons assembled for the Act of Reconciliation, the Cardinal uttered these words : 'God hath given a special token of His favour to this realm, for, as this nation in the time of the Primitive Church was the first to be called out of the darkness of heathendom, so now they were the first to whom God had given grace to repent of their schism' (Fox's *Acts and Monuments,* Vol. VI, p. 572).

Montalembert's appreciation of the British nation and her religion is summed up in the following words : 'After enduring as much and more than any European nation the horrors of religious and political despotism in the sixteenth and seventeenth centuries, she has been the first and the only one among them to free herself from oppression for ever. Re-established in her ancient rights, her proud and steadfast nature has forbidden her since then to give up into any hands whatsoever her rights and destinies, her interests and her free will. In spite of a thousand false conclusions, a thousand excesses, a thousand stains, she is of all modern races and of all Christian nations the one which has best preserved the three fundamental bases of every society which is worthy of man—the spirit of freedom, the domestic character and the religious mind. The Christianity of nearly half the world flows, or will flow, from the fountain which first burst forth upon British soil.'[20]

The Gospel sown by the first Culdees in the soil prepared for it by the labours, over many centuries, of the Druids of Britain, now yields a mighty harvest throughout the English-speaking world.

Travelling swiftly through uncharted periods of Britain's religious history, and up to the Reformation, a mere glance is all that has been possible in this small volume, at some of the outstanding events which have left so indelible a mark upon British character; approach by various avenues has been suggested, any or all of which would lead to illuminating facts in support of lesser-known facts of our history, and to a possible awakening to the responsibilities of a great and ancient heritage.

[1] Green, *Short History of the English People*, Chap. II, p. 83.
[2] Freeman, *Nor. Conq.*, Vol. IV, pp. 434, 435. Hume, *History of England*, Vol. I, p. 361.
[3] Moberly, *Life of Wm. Wykeham*, p. 175.
[4] Hansard, *Parl. Records*, Vol. I, p. 129.
[5] *Governor's Guide*, 8vo., London, 1897.
[6] *Froissart*, Court Chronicles.
[7] J. W. Taylor, *The Coming of the Saints*, p. 175.
[8] *History of Latin Christianity*, Vol. II, p. 234.

[9] *Church History of Britain*, Vol. II, p. 424.
[10] Sismondis, *Hist. Des Francaise*, XVI, 364.
[11] Fox's *Book of Martyrs*, Vol. II, p. 487.
[12] Rev. R. Douglas, M.A., *God and Greater Britain*, p. 125.
[13] Kathleen Brown in *The National Message*, Sept. 27, 1947, p. 302.
[14] Strype, *Annals*, Vol. I, pp. 227, 228.
[15] *Ap. Ch. of England*, Jewel, pp. 13, 14.
[16] Hansard, *Parl. Records*, Vol. I, p. 833.
[17] Life, p. 198.
[18] *Papal Monarchy*, p. 133.
[19] *The Month*, Jan. 1903, p. 3.
[20] *Monks of the West*, Vol. II, p. 367.

INDEX